The Patient as Text

CW00551123

The Patient as Text

the role of the narrator in psychiatric notes
1890–1990

PETTER AASLESTAD
Professor of Scandinavian Literature
Norwegian University of Science and Technology, Trondheim

Translated by
Erik Skuggevik and Deborah Dawkin

This translation has been published with the financial support of NORLA

The support of the Research Council of Norway is gratefully
acknowledged

Radcliffe Publishing
Oxford • New York

Radcliffe Publishing Ltd
18 Marcham Road
Abingdon
Oxon OX14 1AA
United Kingdom

www.radcliffe-oxford.com
Electronic catalogue and worldwide online ordering facility.

British Library Cataloguing in Publication Data

A catalogue record for this book is available from the British Library.

ISBN-13: 978 184619 362 0

The paper used for the text pages of this book
is FSC certified. FSC (The Forest Stewardship
Council) is an international network to promote
responsible management of the world's forests.

Mixed Sources
Product group from well-managed
forests and other controlled sources
www.fsc.org Cert no. SGS-COC-2482
© 1996 Forest Stewardship Council

Typeset by Pindar NZ, Auckland, New Zealand
Printed and bound by TJI Digital, Padstow, Cornwall, UK

Contents

Preface

This book grew out of the desire of a transcultural psychiatrist to learn more about storytelling in order to get a better understanding of his patients' very diverse ways of describing their experience, all of them different according to their cultural backgrounds. The rationale was that improved knowledge about storytelling would lead to the writing of better patient records. I soon discovered that I needed a more thorough knowledge about the genre of the patient file itself, if I was to understand how patients of today, irrespective of cultural background, were portrayed in their records. This led me to study patient files from a psychiatric asylum in Oslo, starting from its early days, 100 years ago, all the way to the present day. A typical academic enterprise, one might scoff: a problem presents itself and the academic takes it upon himself to chart an entire historical development – without answering the question. We never did get as far as the transcultural patients of today. And yet these past records do give us interesting pointers to how patients are represented and given a voice in their files today.

This book was first published back in 1997 and is currently used by a variety of medical training programmes. Both medical and psychology journals commented on the book's relevance in reviews of the revised, second edition that came out in 2007:

> The linguistic analyses of the author show the relevance of a multi-perspective approach to phenomena within psychiatry. Aaslestad's book provides an excellent foundation for reflection on one's own writing, and a chance to become aware of one's own "blind spots" and preconceived ideas both about culture and patient treatment. That is no small accomplishment. *The Patient*

as Text is a refreshing and stimulating book, to be heartily recommended for all psychologists. (*The Journal for The Norwegian Psychological Association.* 2008; **45**(8))

So what is Aaslestad's own narrative like? As a reader I am impressed by a concise, almost elegant style. An excellent work. [. . .]This second edition remains largely unchanged, but contains a new introduction in which the author sets the book within the framework of developments in Medical Humanities and narrative based medicine.

This is set to be a Norwegian classic – an inspiration to colleagues with an interest in research in the Medical Humanities. It ought to be required reading in psychiatry training. Clinicians in other specialist fields, including for example general or internal medicine, will also gain from reading it. This is a book for those of us who write patient files – read it and consider how you describe your fellow beings. (*The Journal of the Norwegian Medical Association.* 2007: **127**: 2268–9)

For some time there have been requests to present this research outside Scandinavia, so that we are now presenting this new English language edition. Thanks are due to the Research Council of Norway and NORLA for their support for this project, and to Cecil Helman who first suggested that I got in touch with Radcliffe.

Petter Aaslestad
October 2009

About the author

Petter Aaslestad is professor at the Norwegian University of Science and Technology in Trondheim. He completed his PhD (1990) at the University of Oslo with a thesis on narrative structures in Norwegian Realism in the nineteenth century. From 1979 to 1992 Aaslestad worked as wetenschappelijk medewerker at the University of Amsterdam. Since 1992 he has held posts at the NTNU in Trondheim, first as Senior Lecturer in Comparative Literature, and since 1994 as Professor of Scandinavia Literature.

From 1999 to 2006 Aaslestad was Dean at the Faculty of Humanities at the University of Trondheim, and from 2002 to 2006 he was Head of the National Conference of Faculties of Arts in the Norwegian Association of Higher Education Institutions. Today he is Chairman of The Norwegian Agency for Quality in Higher Education.

His interest in narrative theory has taken him from studies in French avant-garde literature, via Norwegian Realism to psychiatric patient records. Aaslestad has also written books on Modernism in Norwegian Literature, Samuel Beckett and narratology and has edited, amongst other things, a two-volume collection about the Norwegian Literary Canon.

Author's note

"He" and "his" is generally used to refer to the patient as a role, but this is a choice of convenience, and "he" in this respect applies as much to female as male patients.

Introduction

In the years that have passed since the first edition of *The Patient as Text*, I have often been asked: "What made you begin this project?" It is tempting to answer in measured and professional tones that I wanted, as the subtitle says, to investigate the role of the narrator in psychiatric patient files from Gaustad Hospital through the 100-year period 1890–1990. But of course the reasons for writing any book are always more complex than is evident from the cover. A mix of one's own research interests, a number of coincidences, the zeitgeist, as well as something beyond words, are not uncommon driving factors for academic writing; and thus it was with this project. My initial starting point was my research into two very diverse authors; Samuel Beckett and the Norwegian Jonas Lie. The ability of these two writers to explore the limits of the epic fascinated me. Lie's late nineteenth century novels and Beckett's novels of the latter half of the twentieth both deviated hugely from traditional prose, and yet their stories still didn't collapse. This prompted me to ask: how resilient is the narrative structure of *non-fiction*? But my fascination for the narrative structure of non-fiction did not draw me towards a general investigation of the characteristics of non-fiction, as was the trend in the 1990s. I felt that a deeper exploration of narrative needed to be anchored in a clearly defined textual corpus.

Most important in making this book come about were the conversations I had as a literary critic, with Edvard Hauff as a psychiatrist. We discussed our respective areas of expertise for some time, with no ambition of channelling our dialogue into any particular project. Hauff specialised in transcultural psychiatry, which meant that an understanding of the variation in storytelling patterns of people from different cultures was part of his daily work. At the same time he was frustrated by the fact that patient files often failed to capture things that felt significant to both patient and doctor. Eventually this concern articulated itself into a question: "If health practitioners knew more about storytelling processes, might this result in improved hospital patient files?" This question opened the way to our approaching this field through literary criticism. But to instruct psychiatrists in "how to narrate stories" would, no doubt, have been viewed as impertinent on my part. And without any proper knowledge of current practice or indeed the contents of psychiatric files, I would have been in no position to suggest potential improvements. As luck would have it, we were granted access to the patient files of Gaustad Psychiatric Hospital, thanks partly to Professor Svein Haugsgjerd's interest in the project.

Hauff and I read some patient files together as far back as 1992. Our pilot project indicated that a systematic reading of material covering a substantial period of time, might reveal structures within the writing that were peculiar to the genre of the psychiatric hospital record. For some months I visited Gaustad to read the patient files that I was presented with, according to specific randomised selection criteria. We chose material consisting of around 150 files of patients diagnosed with schizophrenia (previously dementia praecox). The material was limited to the period 1890–1990, partly because we wanted a contemporary focus and intended to link the files with our own time, and partly because the number 100 has a symmetrical beauty. (In retrospect I think it would have been reasonable to take our research from the opening of the asylum in 1856.) Although the most systematic investigation is obviously focused on the period 1890–1990, I have commented on some material from both before and after these dates.

As the material was being gathered, I contributed the occasional lecture for seminars and courses linked to specialist training in psychiatry. The response I received about the project on such occasions influenced my further reading of the files. I was drawn into the hermeneutic cycle, where new partial observations constantly altered the perception of the whole, at the same time as the whole was continuously modified by the reading of ever more patient records, psychiatric history and professional literature on the writing of patient records. It took a long time for the material to be edited and put in the chronological format in which the book now appears. In short, this book came about through a lengthy process, involving many contributors.

Of course, what emerges in these pages is not a complete picture of 100 years of record writing; this book is based on limited cross-sections of a very large body of material. In particular my focus has been on how the patient is given a *voice* and made *visible* in the selected files. Although the developments in the files mapped here may have some value within the history of psychiatry, my prime purpose has been to isolate what is peculiar to the overall genre of the psychiatric patient record. As such the *diachronic* aspect of this study is subservient to the *synchronic*. A greater in-depth knowledge about the characteristics of the genre will make the people writing and reading hospital files more conscious of the potential of the written report. At the same time it will highlight the sorts of pressure the writer undergoes when producing notes, making it easier to identify whether the writer is in command of the text or whether the text steers the writer.

Since this book's publication, I have lectured on this topic in numerous contexts: within psychiatry for both practitioners and service users, and for various humanistic, medical or cross-disciplinary audiences. Seminar participants have overwhelmingly reacted with enthusiasm and curiosity about the use of literary criticism in approaching patient records. I have noticed, however, that over time with the format of the short lecture, which naturally encourages the use of bite-sized examples, some of the book's insights risk becoming locked into "frozen truths". This revised edition offers the opportunity to revisit the more complex, underlying arguments.

Interdisciplinarity is, both as a concept and practice, more common today than when this book was first published in 1997. At the time, I did not feel wholly comfortable about encroaching on other people's disciplines.[1] Not wishing to become a "jack of all trades" (a pitfall risked by anyone venturing into the professional fields of others), and simultaneously not wishing to trivialise my own professional field, I have been careful to comment throughout on my chosen strategies.

Cultural Studies have taken root in the humanities in the period that has passed since this book was first written. And contextual approaches rather than empirical ones have been in the ascendance within literary criticism too. Even within Narrative Theory we see a shift in interest towards the macro levels, at the expense of refining the methodological tools for the close

---

1   Although it was possible to draw inspiration from researchers like Kirsti Malterud (1990), John Nessa (1995) and Ida Hydle (1996), who investigated the doctor–patient relationship in the contexts of communication theory or social anthropology.

reading of texts.[2] This trend is so marked, that one wonders if *The Patient as Text* could have been written today. Yet, in my experience the textual analyses of these patient files, which make up the main thrust of the book, still attract interest and offer new insights for those that come into contact with them. I have tried, as much as is possible, to preserve the textual analysis at the centre in this new edition, without putting too much emphasis on detailed terminology. The literary analysis in the book is more thorough than a lecture situation allows for, but it is certainly not exhaustive. It is hoped that the examples selected for analysis here are suitable for use in discussions about the writing of patient records in various training situations.

This book was a fairly isolated voice when it first appeared, but several Nordic investigations have since referred to *The Patient as Text* as a methodological and theoretical starting point for the analysis of similar material.[3] Today this book can be safely put within what is internationally known now as the Medical Humanities, in which various fields including history, anthropology, linguistics, philosophy, religion and literary criticism, contribute to the development of medical insights.

The concept of *Narrative Based Medicine* is central to the *Medical Humanities*.[4] The tensions between so called "evidence based medicine" and "narrative based medicine" can turn quickly into polemic arguments, and do not belong in our discussion here.[5]

Today, sections of the medical profession, both nationally and internationally, emphasise the capacity of writing itself to aid self-awareness. Fiction is also used in some medical training establishments with the aim of increasing understanding of both the doctor and the patient role.[6] Besides

---

2   Stefan Iversen and Henrik Skov Nielsen observe that present day narratology incorporates terms from feminism, reader response theory, deconstruction and general philosophy, while simultaneously expanding its own field of research (in Aaslestad 1999, p. 11).

3   cf, for instance, Skålevåg SA. *Fra normalitetens historie – Sinnssykdom 1870–1920.* Bergen; 2003; Kirkebæk B. *Letfærdig og løsagtig – kvindeanstalten på Sprogø 1923–1961.* Holte; 2004; Engebretsen E. *Barnevernet som tekst. Nærlesning av 15 utvalgte journaler fra 1950 – og 1980-tallet.* Oslo; 2006.

4   cf the anthology by Greenhalgh T, Hurwitz B (eds). *Narrative Based Medicine. Dialogue and Discourse in Clinical Practice.* London; 2004.

5   Based on experiences in his own practice, Cecil Helman comments on this tension in his book *Suburban Shaman: tales from medicine's frontline.* Hammersmith Press; 2006.

6   Medical students at the University of Oslo attend courses such as "Health and Art". cf Fjellstad K, Isaksen TO, Frich JC. Kunst i den medisinske grunnutdanningen. *The Journal*

which, training in writing skills is used both as a part of patient treatment as well as in various training programmes aimed at increasing medical students' skills of reflection.

The two central theorists that I discovered in the mid-1990s, Kathryn Montgomery Hunter and Rita Charon, who both brought a literary perspective into medical studies, still appear to be at the forefront in the field of Narrative Medicine. In 2006 the former published the book *How Doctors Think: Clinical Judgement and the Practice of Medicine* (now under the name of Kathryn Montgomery). It has little new to offer in relation to our investigative project, but consolidates old insights about the importance of storytelling.[7]

Rita Charon's book *Narrative Medicine: Honoring the Stories of Illness*, published in 2006, emphasises the need for narrative competence among medical practitioners.[8] Charon, who is a doctor herself, trains her students in various narrative skills, showing, for example, how different reading strategies can be transferred to the doctor–patient encounter. Both Charon and Montgomery (Hunter) display sound understanding of the potential in having a solid grasp of the narrative process, and Charon (despite as a doctor coming from outside the field of scientific literary criticism) is particularly well versed in the more recent theories and trends, making her book the most relevant of the two contributions to the field of Narrative Medicine. Yet in the end they both, more or less explicitly, place Narrative Medicine firmly outside the scientific field. In the area of skills training that Charon and Montgomery work within, this may have its understandable, practical justification. Yet, as a practitioner in the human sciences, it is hardly pleasing to find oneself placed outside the *scientific* field. So it is important to remember that this study, which can be placed retrospectively within Narrative Medicine – particularly in view of the impact it has had – actually has its origin in scientific literary criticism.

---

of the Norwegian Medical Association. 2003; **16**: 2316–18; Frich JC. Medisin som litterær virksomhet. *The Journal of the Norwegian Medical Association.* 2003; **17**: 2474–6.

7   Montgomery's view of the importance of narrative may be summed up in the following: "In medicine, narrative is essential for the transfer of clinical knowledge and insight gained from practice" (Montgomery, 2006, p. 49).

8   For her "the narratological" is the starting point for all medicine: "Narrative medicine is a very practical undertaking. It arises from the day-in, day-out events of the doctor's or nurses' office" (Charon, 2006, p. 17).

Prelude

"Suffered a restless night," the doctor quoted from my notes. "No," I answered, "I wasn't restless, I was scared."

These are the words of an anonymous female caller to a radio programme on NRK (Norwegian National Broadcasting), 30 years after a stay in a psychiatric hospital during which she underwent a lobotomy.[9] It is a quote that deserves emblematic status; the two parties, doctor and patient, each approach the medical record from opposite sides, each with their own interpretation of its content. Despite the patient's story being at the very heart of the psychiatric record, the patient does not recognise it as her own – this, quite simply, is what the medical record presents the reader with so often.

This patient went on to describe her overwhelming fear of radiation coming out of the walls, and how she tried to protect herself from it. The description of her behaviour given in her medical notes did not reflect *her* experience, but rather that of the professionals on the ward. This fundamental discrepancy between writer and patient lies at the heart of the genre of the medical note or report. The intense loneliness of the patient experience is evident even in a fragment as neutral and brief as the one above.

A frequently used concept is that of the patient as a *text* and the doctor as a *reader* of that text. This can be a useful image when it comes to understanding

---

9   NRK radio P1, 25/10/1992, following the NRK film *Asylet* [*The Asylum*]. The patient's experiences were from Faret Asylum, Skien, outside Oslo.

some of the complex interpretive processes that take place in the encounter between patient and doctor. The analogy may, of course, appear rather simplistic, but in modern literary criticism the notions of both text and reader are in fact complex and unstable, capable of modifying the strictly one-directional subject–object relationship that many claim characterises the doctor–patient relationship.

My approach to reading the hospital records was partly determined by a *"horizontal"* sender-message-reader model, and partly by a "vertical" multi-layered model where I distinguish between "discourse" as the surface text, and "story" as the underlying reality the narrative refers to. Using concrete examples from various records and patient files we will explore the implications of these ideas, and how knowledge of them can clarify some of the problematic aspects of record writing.

My interest in narratological aspects of texts meant that I had high expectations of the psychiatric records: an insane person's behaviour and their perspective on life is often understood to be an integral part of their illness. It therefore seemed to me that the narrative potential ought to be much greater in psychiatric records than in those that are concerned with illnesses of a more "mechanical" nature, restricted to medical problems in parts of the body. Looking back, however, I realise that the difference is not that great after all: all medical records are essentially narrative in structure; that is, it is impossible to imagine a record that did not describe events through time.

Nonetheless, there are certain peculiarities in psychiatry as a medical science and as a practice that one needs to keep in mind when investigating the narratives of these records and I will deal with these in my next chapter, "Background".

In the following chapter "Departure points" I will outline the practical basis for my investigation of the Gaustad psychiatric records, and also explore the text-theoretical strategies that underpin my analysis of these records. This chapter will function as an introduction to theories and methodology, and will be relevant to fields of study other than psychiatry. Before embarking on our 100-year journey through the Gaustad psychiatric files I will, towards the end of this section, look at a psychiatric report from another psychiatric clinic, Vinderen; Gabriel Langfeldt and Ørnulf Ødegaard's (1978) well-known psychological assessment of Norway's controversial Nazi-sympathising Nobel Laureate in literature, Knut Hamsun. This section is intended as a textual intermezzo of both cultural and historical interest, but it will allow some more general aspects of the hospital record to be discussed.

Our material has been divided into four sections, each dealing with a segment of the period 1890–1990. In the first of these sections, I give considerable attention to the basic writing strategies that run through these notes, not only in the first period of our investigation, but throughout the entire 100-year period. As a consequence this is the longest of the four sections. I intend to focus on both diachronic and synchronic aspects of the material, but in the reading of material from "our own time", to which I have the least historical distance, I will enter into the text more easily as a participant, as both actor and debater. Finally, I will place this research in the wider context of other models of the doctor–patient relationship and the genre of report writing.

1

Background

PAST AND PRESENT

What struck me most during my work was how easily the conditions and ideas contemporary to the psychiatric records leave traces in the text, both in its form and its content. The encounter between doctor and patient, as it emerges in these texts, appears to be governed not only by contemporary scientific doctrine, but also by ideological trends; both popular and elitist attitudes to disease and madness. And on a fundamental level one also senses how society's highs and lows impact on the texts. In his classic *Madness and Civilization* Michel Foucault shows how the perceptions of the mentally ill have changed over time.[10] An accepted part of society in the Middle Ages, the madman gradually took on the role of leper during the Age of Reason, becoming a rejected and isolated figure; the madman becomes an outsider along with others that have fallen by the wayside; the homeless, the work-shy, simpletons and criminals. In the Age of Reason madness had to be demarcated and placed on the *outside*. Rejection of the insane was the price that had to be paid to maintain the rule of reason.

Foucault has been criticised for basing many of his historical conclusions on gross simplifications, as well as for consistently romanticising madness.[11] Foucault's generalisations are, for our purposes, too sweeping for a direct dialogue to be fruitful, added to which, his book belongs absolutely to the 1960s, making application today difficult. However,

---

10 Foucault M. *Madness and Civilization. A History of Insanity in the Age of Reason* (trans. R Howard). Routledge: 1964/1989.

11 For example, McNay L. *Foucault. A Critical Introduction*. Cambridge; 1994, p. 25.

Foucault supplies ample evidence that attitudes are subject to the changes of time, and far more so than the prevailing, positivistic medico-scientific ideal is normally willing to admit. The pervasiveness of ideology will, as I have suggested, shine through the material from Gaustad sometimes with surprising vigour. Yet – and this is significant – the connection between ideology and text is not merely a mechanistic cause-and-effect relationship; the ideologies of *one* period can show up in the notes made in *another*. Thus there is not always a temporal alignment between the contents of the notes and the world at large. For instance, the almost anarchic approach to treatment – the anti-psychiatry of the "out-of-the-asylums" attitudes of the 1960s and 70s – can show up in a later period, but then in the form of an absence of care in the 1990s, where economic priorities take precedence. Thus the idea is realised in a later period, but with very different ideological priorities. This lack of temporal concurrence and the twisting of the meaning of ideas, can clearly distort our historical understanding of the medical record.

FREEDOM AND SUBJUGATION

Humane intentions or optimism about patient recovery can be experienced in diametrically opposite ways: either as a trusting openness or alternatively as invasive and robbing the patient of freedom. Such ambiguity will complicate the analysis of sections of the material from Gaustad Hospital throughout.

In a chapter on the evolution of psychiatry, Professor Einar Kringlen (1977) investigates the so-called "moral treatment" that became fashionable from the 1830s, but which, according to him, faded out as an ideology some thirty years later:

> The idea was that the patient should be treated in small institutions, in some places more like guests, and the policy of the open door was to prevail. The use of coercion was generally done away with. There was often enthusiastic optimism when it came to treatment outcomes. Some asylum directors reported a 90% cure rate. (Kringlen 1977, p. 15)

What is interesting here is the expression of optimism about treatment; this was not the last time in psychiatric history that we see an unequivocal belief that the measures put in place are, finally, the right ones.[12] Kringlen identifies a disparity between what physicians had learned in their training and what they actually expressed in their work:

> It was a common perception at the time that mental illness was on the increase. Despite every doctor "knowing" from their training that insanity was a disorder of the brain, the causes were in practice attributed to factors such as bad health, religious anxiety, failed expectations, financial loss, masturbation and modern civilisation. This environmental theory was particularly prevalent in the USA, where it was assumed mental illness had increased most. The problems lay with the institutions of society, so it was not only urbanisation and technology that came under attack, but the school and family. Schools put too much pressure on the children, families did not teach their children obedience and morality. *The new institutions therefore had a twofold task. They should rehabilitate the sick, but also set an example for the greater community.* (ibid, p. 15f, italics added)

Here, Kringlen points to something that makes the psychiatric report inherently *unstable*; the continually unresolved interaction between the biological and social causal models. Interestingly Kringlen asserts that doctors found themselves unable to practice what they had learned in their medical training, retreating instead to alternative models of understanding in their daily work. There is no reason to assume this was only true of a 30-year period in the nineteenth century; in the Gaustad material we often see individual carers falling back on a "common sense" approach, although this is usually disguised, for example, as psychiatric professionalism. The wisdom of individual careers, as well as its absence, will appear in the notes throughout the 100-year period, in differing magnitude and at unexpected moments.

Even if the ideology of the "moral treatment" dies out around 1860, Kringlen admits that it continues to have some relevance, even in our own time:

---

12 In his *Psykiatriens samtidshistorie* (2001) Kringlen stresses the political significance of the "cure myth" as he calls it: "The asylums were extolled as medical, scientifically founded institutions, characterised by compassion" (p. 27). Not until the 1870s or 80s were these reports of high cure rates subjected to scientific scrutiny.

> Research indicates that a good hospital environment prevents many chronic patients from developing bizarre behaviour and apparent lethargy (Galioni *et al.*, 1953). Visiting different psychiatric institutions it is clear to see that in "inhumane" wards the patients seem very poorly, whilst many schizophrenics in modern hospitals with environmental therapy can seem apparently "normal". The shoring up of psychiatric hospitals over the last 30 years, shares many characteristics with the so-called "moral treatment" in the first part of the last century (Rees, 1957). It is the opinion of many, therefore, that it is difficult to pinpoint the influential component when it comes to the effectiveness of treatment. (Kringlen, 1977, p. 334)

It is interesting that ideas about treatment can resurface 160 years on. This points to the unique place psychiatric thinking occupies within medicine, and in our context, to the complexity of the thinking we will see reflected in the records.

If the patient can seem *less* ill when the environment around him does *not* emphasise his illness – then we surely cross into Foucauldian territory, where the designation of the aberrant is at all times dependent on his/ her *surroundings*. But as we shall see later, these relativistic attitudes can paradoxically only be maintained if they find their counterweight in the hospital's natural and absolute authority.

In the first period after its opening, Gaustad's approach seems influenced by the already waning "moral treatment" of the day:

> From the very outset, an effort was made towards making the asylum, and a stay there, as pleasant as possible [. . .] Already in its first summer an open-air dance floor was built [. . .] On at least one evening a week, every employee, often with their spouse, spent an evening socialising with the patients. There was regular musical entertainment. (Austad, Ødegaard, 1956, p. 131f)

In addition to the social dimension of the treatment, work was also regarded as extremely important. Gaustad's first director, O. Sandberg, stated as early as 1856 that work was the best treatment at the hospital's disposal:

> His statistics show that [. . .] half [were] in regular employment, and over the years this percentage grew. Farm work and gardening in particular were seen as useful activities, and the patients also participated in the daily running of the asylum, in chopping wood, housework etc. (ibid, p. 133)

As a precondition to this apparently generous openness, in which the patients were treated, as far as possible, as though they were well, there was a parallel requirement for *absolute obedience*:

> Gaustad's first regulations [. . .] state that patients should be treated with all the mildness and humanity compatible with their true requirements – and that in return "unconditional compliance" is required of them, according to the relevant regulations. Unwilling or uncooperative patients will burden the management with the onerous duty of using force, straightjackets, isolation etc. but for as limited a period and as sensitively as possible. (ibid, p. 129)

So the generosity we find above is contingent on the unconditional compliance of the patient.[13] Foucault argues that the *deification of the doctor* has been an essential part of the structure of the world of the asylum since the end of the 1700s, and that this deified figure has become instrumental in the modern experience of madness:

> Now [the physician] becomes the essential figure of the asylum. He is in charge of entry [. . .] However [. . .] the doctor's intervention is not made by virtue of a medical skill or power that he possesses in himself and that would be justified by a body of objective knowledge. It is not as a scientist that *homo medicus* has authority in the asylum, but as a wise man. If the medical profession is required, it is as a juridical and moral guarantee, not in the name of science. (Foucault, 1989, p. 256f)

Foucault, incidentally, cites sources similar in content to the quote from Gaustad above. The role of the doctor reflects the fundamental power structures of a patriarchal society:

> [. . .] by wearing the mask of Father and of Judge, that the physician, by one of those abrupt short cuts that leave aside mere medical competence, became the almost magic perpetrator of the cure, and assumed the aspect of a Thaumaturge; it was enough that he observed and spoke, to cause secret

---

13 It is useful here to revisit Foucault for an understanding of this apparently paradoxical attitude. I came to Foucault's ideas on this subject later in my work, having only had a fleeting knowledge of *Madness and Civilization* when I started. But his ideas give weight to some of the more sweeping generalisations in this book.

> faults to appear, insane presumptions to vanish, and madness at last to yield to reason. (ibid, p. 259f)

The early requirement for absolute obedience, as set down in Gaustad's first regulations, finds its roots in this understanding of the doctor's role, which according to Foucault has been venerated since the mid-eighteenth century. This brings us closer to understanding the inherent contradictions that must have characterised life in the asylums, and which we will see again in later material. The moral position that both patient and doctor adopt, to ensure the necessary deference to the father figure, is not perceived as such, but as a mark of respect for the objectivity of science.

This beautiful and nostalgic picture of those first years at Gaustad, in the spirit of the vanishing "moral treatment" with its dance evenings on the open-air stage and its outside work, was firmly underpinned by the impossibility of questioning the asylum's superior and unshakeable authority. Should one, as an individual, not fit into the collective spirit, both the pleasant social activities and the meaningful work would rapidly be replaced by something opposite – something *unpleasant* and *meaningless*. Thus the opposite side of this freedom, constantly latent, is exposed:

> Thus we can [. . .] conclude that the principle in the institution was acclimatising and disciplining, and that this, amongst other things, was made possible by isolation and confinement. Or, in other words: the psychiatric institution and its science offered its patients treatment, and this treatment was tantamount to social control. (Kelstrup, 1977, p. 93)

Kelstrup uses Amalie Skram's *Professor Hieronimus* as an example. This novel, written by the celebrated Norwegian novelist after her stay in Copenhagen's County Hospital in 1894, offers a satirical portrayal of her doctor, Professor Pontoppidan, in the shape of Hieronimus. The female protagonist lacks, according to the professor, *any capacity for discipline*. For this reason, she will be locked up "by the mechanical route" for a year. The first six months will be spent protesting. Thereafter, she will calm down and finally leave the hospital, a grateful person.

The lazier and less socially minded amongst us – for whom the idea of being involved with a school jumble sale is stretching it – will, irrespective of our mental health, sympathise with the discomfort of submitting to such rigid demands of submission to the work and leisure activities for the common good. The sense of humiliating subjugation that Skram writes about in *Professor Hieronimus* may in her case, of course, spring from deeper sources, but her example says something about the difference between the hospital's intentions and the individual patient's experience. This need not even have its basis in any deliberate desire to abuse power, which according to more simplistic psychiatric criticism, is the dominant motivation of carers.

SOCIAL CLASS AND PATHOLOGY

A patient like Amalie Skram would probably, had she been admitted to Gaustad in its early years, have benefited from the greater understanding of her individuality. Particularly since the first regulations not only divided patients according to categories of illness, but adapted treatment to social background.

Mr Herman Wedel Major, involved in the planning of Gaustad, proposed the following to the Government of the day:

> First Class for the Calm and Decently behaved [. . .]
>
> Second Class for Patients that [. . .] are unsuited for communal living and troublesome to others.
>
> Third Class for the noisy, violent, obstinate and dangerously ill.
>
> Fourth Class for those befallen to unclean and immoral behaviour.
>
> Additionally another reason for division should be taken into consideration; the different educational levels of patients, since between those who have received careful upbringing and scientific learning from childhood, and those from the unmannered sections of the populous, there exists such a substantial difference in respect of their accustomed lifestyles and expectations of personal comfort, that it would be equally unfortunate and unnatural for either group, if one were to bring them under uniform conditions with respect to accommodation, diet, and social and professional activities. (Retterstøl, 1995, p. 19)

Does this imply that those of a certain social standing move up one class on the illness scale? The quote is interesting, not as an exposé of social differentiation, but as an example of how the pathological and the social dimensions are continually interwoven in the patient's interaction with the hospital. This reflects the same structure that Foucault identified during the Age of Reason's segregation of people who were, for various reasons, considered deviant. Thus, illness and social status become inseparable. I mention this not in order to make any outlandish suggestions that insanity does not exist, but to suggest that the psychiatric records will be influenced by factors that are often far removed from the strictly medico-scientific field. Neither is there is any reason to assume that this is not the case in more recent times too.

Acknowledging this complexity, and the difficulty of isolating specifically psychiatric elements, let me point to a somewhat despairing comment on psychiatric training made by Johan Scharffenberg in the Journal of the Norwegian Medical Association (1908, 461–70), in which he ridicules the slapdash attitude of the legal system to the appointment of psychiatric experts, as well as the slowness of medical establishment in providing competent instruction in psychiatry. The prevailing attitude, he concludes bitterly, seems to be that "one needs nothing more than 'common sense to diagnose and treat insanity'" (ibid, p. 467). Such "common sense" appears in the psychiatric records throughout our 100 years of material, and psychiatry itself has clearly been part of shaping it.

THE NOTE-WRITER IN SOCIETY

The attitudes of one historical époque can be seen to lie latent only to break out again in reports at different times. And in any one historical moment we can find opposite attitudes to the same phenomenon. Something that appears caring and considerate in one period may look like extreme abuse seen from another angle. And vice versa. For example the major abuses, as we see them today, lobotomy being the prime example, were in their own time seen as offering the only hope of improvement in an impossible situation.

The history of the psychiatric report resists any linear narrative. There is no plot offering grand arrows of progression; beginning in ignorance, superstition and barbarism, passing through the vanquishing of the limitations of the past, culminating in the eventual insights of our own time.

More than in other area in medicine, it seems that historical context and intellectual climate of the wider society is crucial in the understanding of psychiatric illness. It seems to me then, that the writer of these patient notes should ideally have the facility to reflect on sociological and historical conditions. This may seem like a huge, unrealistic demand, but it is no different in essence to that made by us of other *writers of texts*. Which brings us to the final complicating factor in understanding the process of writing psychiatric notes. During the 100-year period under investigation, the relationship to the written word has itself shifted. As the presentation of reports has become increasingly sophisticated – steadily gaining a more organised appearance, passing from handwriting, to typewriter, to word processor – health personnel have lost their skills as writers of social texts.

Once upon a time, a doctor was automatically someone who could write well. The systematically composed report developed into a genre during the eighteenth century, alongside newspaper writing and the modern novel. The doctor was one of many who participated in the production of cultural discourse. Those entering the health professions now, rarely possess such a culturally prominent role. That said, this does not mean that they cannot regain it!

2

Departure points

MEETING THE TEXT

Throughout the years, writers of medical notes can hardly have expected *literary critics* to be among their potential readers. In my first encounter with the patient records at Gaustad I had the unpleasant feeling that I was becoming a *voyeur*. Interest in closed psychiatry is – among nobler motives – also motivated, no doubt, by the less acceptable thrill of peeping in on what others keep hidden. The sense of shame for my voyeuristic activity waned as the triviality of the patient notes revealed itself, and as my understanding of their actual content grew. My focus soon shifted to its proper area: the study of writing itself. I quickly discovered a huge divergence; that is, that even in the production of patient notes, we find a difference between good and bad writers, despite the fact that the demand for originality and stereotypes differs from other genres. A writer's warmth, ignorance, lack of manners, empathy, self-righteousness, humour or self-criticism, all leave traces, almost independently of the record's medical content.

The record-writer is at the service of many people, and even nowadays numerous voices often pass, mostly anonymously, through him; these might include ward nurses, ergotherapists, wardens, the manager of the sewing room, psychologists, hospital nurses, even the gardener for a period, and of course the social worker. All these affect the textual choices of the writer. The hospital record is kept a secret from the outside public, but at the same time it holds within it the entire heterogeneous hospital community. Set against this backdrop, my presence as a reader starts to seem less intrusive than it did when I opened those first records.

It did not take long to see that the fundamental format of the record has remained virtually unchanged: a record opens with the transcribed notes from the authority responsible for submitting the patient; a report then follows of the patient's behaviour during the first 24 hours; then, after a few days, a "Status Praesens" is entered; after which there will follow sporadic, fairly random notes up to the point of discharge.

The patient's background, problems and behaviour are rarely presented in such a way as to be incomprehensible for the outsider. This does not acquit the texts of their potential to manipulate. There are of course numerous seemingly neutral, "innocent" text passages designed to activate certain pre-programmed reactions in the reader.

But where was the patient's voice in the record? And when it was included, when did that voice seem unmediated? These were the basic questions that determined my reading. My task was to read with "other" eyes. Nonetheless, I needed a rudimentary knowledge of the communication that was intended before I could adopt any critical position and mark my detachment from the text.

The oldest texts were the easiest; the line between the individual's suffering and the degree of fictionalisation in the text did not appear disruptive to my analysis. The time lapse between the moment of writing and the act of reading made it safe for me to give myself over to the enjoyment of old-fashioned names, outdated occupational titles etc. – a very different experience from the reading of more recent texts, where the descriptions of recognisable surroundings and people made the uncomfortable, shameful sense of voyeurism rear its intrusive head again.

Glimpses of seamstresses, apprentice bakers, seamen's widows, crofters' daughters, the occasional rentier, contemporary oil workers and students – alongside fluctuations in financial and political trends and events at home and abroad – surface with greater or lesser clarity, only to disappear again. Anxieties over miasmic radiation and invisible electricity fade only to be replaced with anxieties about radioactive effects and impending natural disaster. Against this background of arbitrary and shifting history, there appears a kind of constant – that of individual sickness. It is impossible, during a cross-historical reading, not to feel sympathy for the actual suffering of the patients in their environment. And since no ultimate solution to the treatment of psychiatric illness has been found in any period, sympathy also goes out to society in general and its generally futile attempts at alleviating the pain; a sympathy accompanied, of course, by more familiar feelings of rage and despair at the ignorance and abuses to which patients are, to vary-ing degrees, exposed.

I have tried to offer some insight into the considerations that informed my early readings of the Gaustad material. There is no reason to hide the fact that as a textual analyst this project gave me enormous reading enjoy-ment. Empathy, compassion, shyness, voyeurism and rage were all aspects of the enjoyment born out of meeting these records, reactions that were generally reined in through my analytical work. I mention this here, since it has struck me that much of the existing interpretive work on medical records reveals a serious lack of understanding of the *instability of the reader*. This ultimately results in a lack of scientific credibility. Yet even the most professional "reader" might, consciously or subconsciously, react to signals within the text that might not be the most pertinent to the research in hand: rather than blaming the text itself for its multiplicity, it is simpler to admit that the reader's role is, by definition, multifaceted.

DISCOURSE AND STORY

My starting point in this analytical work has been the *discourse*, defined as the running text, as it is found written in a record. *The story*, defined as the content referred to in this discourse, becomes that which is, to a greater or lesser degree (although never completely), recoverable from the discourse. The focus of my research is "the story *about* the patient and his illness" *not* "the patient and his illness". Meanwhile, the writer's *starting point* was altogether different from mine; for him, the "true" story gave birth to the written discourse, rather than the other way around. But it is important to stress that this is his "starting point" and that the writer will constantly be in a position of writing according to the narrative structures in which he is entrenched. The writer is doing two things at once: he analyses an object, but also expresses himself through a discourse which might fol-low alternative paths from those primarily indicated by an analysis of the object.

Behind the conceptual dichotomy of discourse/story lies a long history of critical debate in the twentieth century. The debate has revolved around the problematic relationship between reality and the linguistic portrayal of this reality.[14] It is tempting perhaps to use EM Forster's (1960) differentiation

---

14 The distinction of the Russian Formalists between "fibula" and "zujet" and Forster's

of story and plot for our purposes: "First the king died and then the queen died." This, we are told by Forster, is a prime example of *story*, whilst "first the king died and then the queen died *of grief*", is defined as *plot*. A causal link has been established which is absent in the story, which elevates the plot into something more than a referential and chronological listing of events.

The reason I prefer to stay relatively close to French Narratology, and Gérard Genette's distinction between discourse (récit) and story (histoire) is, in part, because of the consistent and fundamental order Genette operates within. Looking more closely at Forster's story/plot distinction, we find it is not as clear-cut as a first reading of his fascinating example might suggest: in the first example, the selection of the queen's death to follow that of the king's, from the myriad alternative possibilities, reveals an organising narrative entity that is essentially no different from the internal causality in Forster's plot. In our material, we frequently encounter examples similar to Forster's "story", in which the writer presents actions in the narrative with no causal indicators, but which can nonetheless be interpreted as a full plot, for example: "After the lobotomy the patient is no longer unclean." Should the patient fall back into old ways later, the writer can hide behind the fact that he was merely keeping chronological record of events. If the improvement persists, the plot can be developed further in the direction of the silent triumph the writer has discreetly laid the path for. Thus, it seems to me that Forster's story is also a plot, and that both are played out on the level of discourse.

The fact that this running text is taken as an object for research, means that the *story* can only be inferred as a construct arising from this text – and not the other way around. This is necessarily the starting point for literary criticism, and it is useful in the mapping of the rhetorical aspects of the text. Yet this is an easier position to maintain in reading older records than recent ones, where the patient may actually be in the next room. In such a situation, the patient's suffering becomes more pressing than the text that describes it – and my interest in interpreting the text, as well as my ability to do so, dulls. And in the most disturbing records that deal, for example, with preventable suicides, it may be convenient to adopt the same obscuring

---

distinction between story and plot are important contributions. The distinction between components as they are in reality and components as they are depicted linguistically can be traced back to Aristotle's notion of the fable in his book about the art of poetry.

and unassuming silence that the note-writer has so often chosen as his strategy.

SENDER VERSUS RECEIVER

Gradually, with increased experience in reading these documents, I lost the distance that I had initially had to the narrative; at times I found myself entering the role of the note-writer and would sometimes pre-empt their conclusions. "Recommend move to Ward D" I thought as I read a note, which indeed concluded with "move to ward D". In such cases the text had imparted its logic to me to such a degree that distance vanished. As a reader I had the text *inside* me, ahead of its existence. In other words I had become not just a text *receiver*, but a text *producer* – of a text identical to the official Gaustad psychiatric record.

Amongst other things, the hospital report is a text that restarts over and over again, in the form of short fragments. The choices a writer makes in the opening phase of a report are decisive of the way in which the text will develop subsequently. This leads us theoretically towards an area of post-structuralism which targets an exploration of textual production itself.

Roland Barthes suggests that all text is merely a new weave of old quotes, and this is indeed clearly illustrated in a genre like the hospital report, with its countless standardised formulations. Throughout the entire material – 100 years of writing – there is tension between the *standardised formulas of the genre* and literary borrowings on the one side, and the quest for *individual expression* on the other.

It is essential that a scholarly reader who sets out to describe the genre of the hospital record maintains an *inquisitive attitude* throughout his reading. However, as I have previously said, it can happen that as a reader I sometimes assimilate the logic of the text to such an extent that I anticipate its turns. In such situations the reading occupies the problematics of transference as discussed by Shoshana Felman in her seminal article "Turning the Screw of Interpretation", which is a representative example of thinking in psychoanalytically inspired literary criticism. Felman highlights the *intersubjective play* which takes place in any act of communication (and particularly in psychoanalysis), and shows how the sender, text and receiver in Henry James' short story "The Turn of the Screw" dissolve as separate concepts. The reader's analysis of the text also implies the text's analysis of itself as well as the text's analysis of the reader. This may sound very jargon-laden, but we will see examples of similar mechanisms of transference during the reading of our records. At times it will be extremely difficult to make a clear differentiation between reader, text and sender, and the concepts will often overlap, or even replace each other. We will be looking at this closer "on location" in the material.

Astonishingly perhaps, the actual content of the discourse of the mentally ill patient was given little analytical attention until the 1970s. The patient's voice is recorded in detail in some periods, and ignored in others, but rarely commented upon.

As an extension of Roland Barthes' textual theories it seems logical to turn to Julia Kristeva's (1991) investigation of the signification processes of language. Kristeva differentiates between what she calls *semiotic* and *symbolic* elements of signification. This distinction may help us to identify some of the problems that the writer has in recording the voice of the psychotic. Borrowing from Lacan, Kristeva differentiates between intersubjective, symbolic language, such as "the Law" and "the Father", parts of a shared language that individuals in a linguistic community have to adhere to; and the semiotic, pre-linguistic field. The pre-linguistic babble of infants, as well as the voice of the psychotic, is purely semiotic, whereas scientific discourse, for example, is virtually devoid of the semiotic, being a purely symbolic language. What is interesting here is that Kristeva sees the two positions (or fields) as simultaneously present in language. All discourse will often experience a push by the semiotic dimension on the symbolic dimension of language. The hospital notes of the schizophrenic will, as we shall see, show an opposite tendency: the pressure of symbolic language trying to keep the semiotic field at bay. Maybe there are such strong defensive strategies at play here, that the language of the psychiatric note is forced into a rigid authoritarian position, more rigid than any other linguistic register in society.

NARRATIVE THEORY AND NON-LITERARY RESEARCH FIELDS
Since the 1980s other disciplines have *covetously* eyed the methodologies of literary criticism. Yet we would be wrong to think that this is a completely new development. Rather we should remind ourselves that studies of rhetoric, once so central to nineteenth century science, were squeezed into a marginalised position; what we are witnessing is the restoration of a

balance that was unsettled with the rise of positivism. It is important, then, that we see today's linguistically based literary criticism as closely related to studies in rhetoric.

Here, I lean on one of the foremost representatives of the New Historicism, Hayden White, who, in a footnote to an article from 1989, gives the following description of the place of rhetoric in the nineteenth century:

> Prior to the early nineteenth century, historiography was regarded as a branch of oratorical discourse and a proper subject of the theory of rhetoric. It was, however, disengaged from rhetoric in the course of the nineteenth century as a result of the movement to render historical studies more scientific. The twofold attack on rhetoric, from Romantic poetics, on the one side, and Positivist philosophy, on the other, led to the general disparagement of rhetoric throughout Western high culture. (White, 1989, p. 41)

Thus, historical research became more scientific as it distanced itself from rhetoric! How very different from the conceptual model of today in which everything is discourse, text and language. Seen from our time, nineteenth century historical research takes, in White's interpretation, a tragic position: a noble pursuit of absolute knowledge undermining itself by vigorously removing any linguistic traces.

Hayden White also points to an overall lack of appreciation of rhetoric within contemporary historical research. There has been a tendency to ignore a number of what White regards as "self-evident" truths; for example, that "history" is only accessible through language, which means our historical experience cannot be separated from our discourse about it.[15]

There is no need for us to adopt a stance on White's postulates on the links between history and language in general, but his views clearly have a bearing on our research. After all, our object of study is 100 years of report *writing*. Our object is itself linguistic. In discussing the relationship between "discourse" and "story" I have emphasised how each individual hospital

---

15 "[. . .] that the 'history' [. . .] is accessible only by the way of language, that our experience of history is indissociable from our discourse about it, that this discourse must be written before it can be digested as 'history', and that this experience, therefore, can be as various as the different kinds of discourse met with in the history of writing itself. On this view, 'history' is not only an object we can study and our study of it, but is also and even primarily a certain kind of relationship to 'the past' mediated by a distinctive kind of written discourse." (ibid, p. 19)

report has been studied for its linguistic content, with no intention of evaluating the reality of the patient or his illness. Even if we do not sign up to all of White's arguments, we may nonetheless find them useful at a more general level of our analysis; my research contributes to the history of psychiatry, but its central object – even empirically – is linguistic. Any attempt to locate the truth behind these stories would, in this context, constitute an impossible project.

MEDICINE AND NARRATIVE

There is clearly a fascination for the methods of literary criticism in today's scientific discourse. I had assumed that my Gaustad research would start me off in the direction of an unwieldy corpus of professional literature. But as I began reading medical literature related to the field of narratology, I was relieved to find that it was easier than I expected to sift out what was truly relevant to my line of investigation.[16]

In this chapter I limit myself to one central publication: Kathryn Montgomery Hunter's (1991) *Doctor's Stories. The Narrative Structure of Medical Knowledge*. Hunter, who has taught medical students in Humanities at American universities since the middle of the 1970s, is an authority in her field. In this investigation she deals mainly with non-psychiatric illnesses. Not limiting herself to the stories found within medical reports, Hunter investigates a wide variety of "doctor's stories" as told in the hospital environment, including the oral anecdote. Independently of each other – and consulting rather different material – Montgomery Hunter and myself have, interestingly, arrived at many of the same fundamental conclusions. Montgomery Hunter emphasises the close connection that exists between medicine and interpretive studies, and soon arrives at the metaphor "the patient as a text". She is sufficiently familiar with poststructuralist thinking to be fairly quick to problematise the dimension of the sender of the text in a way similar to that discussed above:

> The metaphor of the patient as a text and the physician as a well educated, attentive close reader of that text goes a long way toward capturing the complexities of the emotional and epistemological relation between the

---

16 The considerable volume of literature that touches on the narrative in psychoanalysis falls outside the remit of this project, likewise various types of "speech-act" analyses.

physician and the patient. But the medical reading is not a causal or passive one. *The idea of physician as reader and interpreter may be pushed a bit farther, for late twentieth-century literary criticism has taught us that the relationship between author and reader is fully as complex as that between patient and physician.* (Montgomery Hunter, 1991, p. 12, italics added)

Montgomery Hunter does not, however, develop this model very far, and her poststructuralist position seems somewhat superficial and ill integrated. Interestingly, the lessons that Montgomery Hunter suggests we have learned from literary criticism seem, from my perspective, to be the reverse. Through empirical investigation of a non-literary corpus, without any predetermined methodology, I arrive at a problematisation of the sender and receiver relationship, not unlike the one Montgomery Hunter locates in poststructuralist *theory*. The fact that practice and theory seem to confirm one another in two separate investigations hopefully gives added significance to the proceedings we will go on to undertake.

"The patient as a text", as Montgomery Hunter and other literary-medical theorists have conceptualised it, has as its corollary "the doctor as a reader". In our context this is otherwise. Indeed, the use of the concept "the patient as a text" in our research is barely metaphorical. This is because the written records form the *actual* basis for our investigation. Our focus is precisely the "story about the patient". The texts, in our framework, are the result of a meeting between doctor and patient, and as readers we are not looking at "the patient as a text" but rather "the doctor–patient text about the patient". The implications of viewing the doctor–patient relationship as analogous to the reader–text relationship, will be revisited in my final chapter.

Montgomery Hunter demonstrates that it is the unusual and unexpected cases that make primary subjects for narration: "Where success is expected it is not a criterion of narratability" (1991, p. 69). The "average sufferer" is given the least narrative attention. Montgomery Hunter highlights the many anecdotes that fill the world of the hospital ward:

In the midst of a highly technologized, scientific profession, the anecdote is a clear reminder of the fundamental nature of medicine's "raw-material", the exigencies of the particular illness. (ibid, p. 70)

Fundamentally, there is a paradoxical relationship between the general and the uniquely individual. Clinical studies aimed at advancing the scientific understanding of illnesses are based on a large number of cases, whereas stories revolve around unique cases, claims Montgomery Hunter (revealing as she does a poor appreciation of narratology, which we will leave to one side for now). Her point is that stories, as such, appear non-scientific. In our time, doctors have a tendency to treat individual stories as leftover from an uninformed, pre-scientific age, says Montgomery Hunter. Yet the paradox is that medicine is brimming with stories. The treatment of a patient begins with "the patient telling a story while the physician listens" (ibid, p. 72).

Montgomery Hunter is the first to admit that in this harmonious archetypal situation, the equality between storytelling patient and listening doctor is in truth both complex and heterogeneous and, in reality, a myth. It is enough to mention here that in the present day these two parties have drawn closer to each other, without this being entirely in the patient's interest. Western societies have adapted the medical-scientific jargon to a large degree, and the patient now *reads* himself and his symptoms through scientific and medical terminology, and consequently presents his doctor with a story coloured with medical terminology. The doctor is, in other words, responsible for a greater part of the patient's story than a traditional sender-receiver model should imply. In our material from the 1980s and 1990s, for instance, we find patients themselves describing their mental state as "psychotic", and giving detailed descriptions of their experiences based on their preconceptions of a medical understanding of their condition.

The problem associated with the balance of these two different voices – that of patient and doctor – can also work in the opposite way from a psychiatric point of view. The psychiatric patient's speech includes a worldview mixed with psychopathological manifestations, which it falls to the note-writer to record, whilst simultaneously maintaining his observational distance. Instead of the patient's subservience in adopting the language of the other, we can detect a resistance in the writer to giving a faithful record of the dialogue.

These complicating factors are central to text production processes and pre-date the writing of the record. So as not to get bogged down in preliminary ideological speculations about the asymmetry of the doctor–patient relationship, I will revisit some elementary narratology and isolate the voices we primarily and formally encounter in narrative written texts.

WHO IS TELLING?

Since the early 1970s a great deal of research has been done in the field of narratology into the function of the storyteller. We do not need for our purposes to construct a large terminological apparatus, so long as we realise that the question "Who tells?" will produce many complex answers. Not infrequently we will observe in looking at these records that what is presented as the voice of the patient reveals itself to be that of the writer. Conversely, the patient's language can take over the voice of the storyteller for long stretches of text, with or even without the writer's knowledge. Many of the choices connected to the identity of the narrator's voice will reveal themselves to be carriers of veiled ideological messages. Our overall goal must surely be that today's record writers will – through the following analysis – gain greater awareness of the possibilities of different narrative choices. I intend, throughout, to use concrete examples rather than offering theoretical postulates.

My analyses of these texts will rarely pretend to be exhaustive; other readers may doubtless wish to stress alternative aspects of these psychiatric notes and records.[17]

In narratological analysis of fictional writing one has to distinguish between the *author* (the physical person outside the text) and the *narrator* (the entity who tells the story). In contemporary novels in particular, the figure of a narrator is often intentionally different from the actual author himself. The narrator can be *overt* – referring directly to him/herself and his act of narration, or *covert*. It is, however, crucial to recognise that such a narrator does exist, even when he does not take part in the action as a person, or leave any trace in the text by referring to himself in the first person or by reporting on the context within which the writing takes place. In the narrative text we also tend to distinguish between the *narrator* and the person, persons or objects that are the subject of the narrative. The narrator may at times lend his voice to one of the characters. The way in which this is done is complex, but in theoretical terms it may look quite simple: the voices of characters can be given either *directly* or *indirectly*. An example of direct speech: "He said: 'I am travelling tomorrow.'" Or indirect speech: "He said that he was going to travel tomorrow." The indirect speech has "changed" the verb in

---

17 Since the fragments and commentaries in this book might be useful as points of reference for discussion, they have been numbered.

the clause from present to past tense (tense shift) and the pronoun is moved from first person in direct speech to third person in indirect speech. In both cases the "speaking" is seen as an object to the finite verb "said", but in this indirect speech example, the speaking is incorporated into a sub-clause (introduced by "that"). The form "he said" in direct speech is plain narrative text, whereas the quote is personalised text. In indirect speech the entire phrase is the narrator's text. The choice between direct and indirect speech therefore signals an unequal distribution of text belonging to the patient and the writer. This may not sound overly complicated, yet what is peculiar is that we will discover some variants of speech recording in the material rarely found elsewhere. For example, quotation marks are used to indicate the direct speech of patients, yet throughout the entire 100-year period it appears extremely hard for the writers to allow the patient to be represented through the use of the word "I", which is what one would normally expect linguistically.

I make no distinction here between direct and indirect *speech* and direct and indirect *thought*. The difference between "he said" and "he thought" relates to content, and has no formal implications. However, it is usual to include a third type of speech documentation in narrative texts, the so-called free indirect style (often named after its French and German origins; *style indirect libre* or *erlebte Rede*). The statement "He said, 'Sure, I'm going tomorrow!'" might be rendered as follows: "Sure, he was going tomorrow!" Here we find the tense shifts and changes to the personal pronoun, as in indirect speech above, yet the most significant aspect is perhaps the omission of quotation marks. Additionally, the spoken register remains intact: "Sure" from the quote and the exclamation mark indicates a tone of speech. In Norwegian literature, we recognise this style especially from the middle of the nineteenth century, through Asbjørnsen and Moe's folk tales, but it is a style frequently used in literary realism too. If a person's thoughts are reported in longer text segments in this style one speaks of an inner monologue. It was, however, Gustave Flaubert in *Madame Bovary* who really developed the style's potential: Emma Bovary's banal thoughts were related, in part, as a type of inner monologue, but in a sophisticated vocabulary belonging to the narrator, thus creating an ironic effect that lies latent in the style. When free indirect speech is used in this way, it is impossible to distinguish clearly between the narrator's and the character's voice. Free indirect speech can be confused with, or look identical to, indirect speech without any attribution, or simply plain narrative text. Unsurprisingly, there are occasional debates in literary criticism concerning the definitions of this style, and its function and textual significance.

We will see that the writer frequently makes use of free indirect speech in our material. It is a form that seems ideally placed to give an intimate, close-up picture of the patient, while maintaining the necessary distance to him/her, yet without the linguistic signals giving the appearance of being so manipulated that the writer could be understood to be taking an ironic stance. In our research into the way patients are given a voice, we will investigate the various ways the record writer separates the patient's narrative and his own observations. Choice of discursive forms (such as indirect speech, free indirect speech and plain narrative text with quotations) and methods of attribution will be interpreted beyond their purely linguistic paradigms, and contextual factors will be highlighted during our analysis.

Not all patients' voices can be identified as easily as the above outline might suggest. We have already touched on how textual production may be governed by the patient's relationship to medical science, or by the relationship of the writer to the patient's cognitive universe. The stories of both patient and doctor have in that sense been pre-coded before their actual recording. Occasionally, the writer may even consciously or unconsciously reveal aspects of the patient's cognitive universe through his choice of words in what is otherwise a neutral text.

In his chapter "Le plurilinguisme dans le roman" in *Esthétique et théorie du roman* (1978), Mikhail Bakhtin elaborates a frequently undervalued theory concerning the "linguistic zones" of fictional characters, which become mixed with the discourse of the narrator. On a formal level we are dealing with a straightforward narrative, but one that is formulated in such a way that the linguistic paradigms of the fictional characters nonetheless influence the text. This may sound like a description of the aesthetics of modernist literature (e.g. Joyce), but Bakhtin argues that the phenomenon was already evident in the nineteenth century's realist novels, long before any more deliberate experimentation with discursive forms. In the genre of report writing, it might be useful to see whether the "linguistic zone" of the patient spreads into the discourse of the narrator, whether it weakens or possibly replaces it, and the extent to which this is outside the writer's control. If Bakhtin's theory is relevant to our non-fiction texts, it may mean that the patient "has a voice" in textual passages that are, in principle, devoid of his/her formal presence.

THE CORPUS

The textual material consists of 150 patient files from Gaustad Psychiatric Hospital covering approximately the last 100 years, where schizophrenia has been the diagnosis (previously "dementia praecox"). Schizophrenia is the chosen focus of this study, in part because the term has been in regular use for large stretches during this period. Additionally, communication problems are of such relative severity for schizophrenia patients that the issues of narrativity become particularly relevant.[18]

The files were selected for analysis on the basis of set randomisation principles. Allowances have been made to ensure an even spread during the period as well as an even distribution of male and female patients. The textual work itself at Gaustad Hospital took the shape of careful transcriptions of sections from the records (naturally within dispensations given by the Norwegian Directorate for Health).[19] Numerous narratological and content-related factors have, however, played their part, consciously or subconsciously, in the selection process of fragments. I should also mention that there was aversion to, or attraction to, various graphological elements. The handwriting of the 1930s, for instance, was far less appealing to the eye than that from the turn of the nineteenth century. However, the selection of the segments is primarily informed by the premise: how are patients' stories relayed in the hospital? I have attempted to make my selection as multi-faceted as possible.

Since the corpus covers a 100-year period, a significant section of records use the older diagnostic term "dementia praecox". A question that must be asked is whether the diagnosis itself affects the writing of the patient notes? Did the new term, schizophrenia, with its changed perceptions of the illness, also result in another writing style?

The German psychiatrist Emil Kraepelin called one of several psychotic illnesses *dementia praecox*, on account of the patient's age when the illness manifested itself (between 16 and 30 years of age) and the subsequent fast deterioration in intellectual, emotional and social capacity (from Latin

---

18 It should be stressed that I am not attempting to explore the inherent textual structures of the delusions themselves, as, for example, in Rosenbaum and Sonne (1979).

19 The dispensation from the Directorate of Health stipulates among other things that "the patient will not be contacted by the researcher; that the right to privacy in accordance with [regulations] are respected; that private information is kept confidential; that information that might identify any individual is deleted at the end of the project; that the publication of the research makes it impossible to identify any individual."

dementia: *de* = away, and *mens* = mind; "to be away from one's mind"). In other words, Kraepelin emphasised the degenerative nature of the illness, its ability to lead to the young patient's rapid decline towards a condition of *demens*. Should the *demens* not occur, the diagnosis would have to be regarded as wrongly applied. I am referring here to the work of Jean-Pierre Olié and Christian Spadone: *Les nouveaux visages de la folie* (1993).[20]

It was in 1911 that Eugen Bleuler, a student of Kraepelin, introduced the new term schizophrenia (from Greek: *schizein* = cleave, and *phren* = mind; "cleaved mind"), thus stressing the absence – or rather the loss – of a mental wholeness. This loss of wholeness can lead to incoherence, both on the psychological level and in physical behaviour. By rejecting the term *demens* Bleuler indirectly recognised that there were intellectual and emotional resources still present in the disoriented patient; the schizophrenic patient had, in other words, become a person unable to access their potential.

Olié and Spadone point out that people were familiar with Freud's theories in 1911. Thanks to Freud one could assume the existence of an active life of the subconscious, which remained operational even if the patient's conscious processes were disturbed. Behind the psychotic symptoms there were therefore, according to Bleuler, ideas, desires, dreams and imagining that were worth investigation. Kraepelin had highlighted the destructive nature of psychosis. Bleuler rediscovered that which even psychosis cannot eradicate: a "hidden" psychological life, which it was paramount to recognise and explore.

It is hard to believe that the substantial differences between these two concepts, dementia praecox and schizophrenia, did not have some effect on the writing of patient notes. I have often been surprised by how rarely the writers have entered into the thinking of their patients in these notes. Perhaps the old mindset of the illness as "dementia praecox" lingered on long after the term had gone out of use in Norway?

In the perception of this illness as premature dementia, there is a strong element of irreversibility, which incidentally accords well with such a strong

---

20 It has not been possible to compare this (doubtless over-simplified) presentation of Kraepelin's diagnostics with the way Norwegian psychiatrists understood the term at the time. This would not, in fact, have been necessary for our purposes: not because further insight into Kraepelin's view on psychosis is of no interest, but because our interest here is how the diagnosis itself might have influenced the writing of patient records.

belief amongst the Norwegian medical community in a scientific cause-and-effect model. Consequently there are two things from Bleuler that are of particular note. Firstly, the idea of the Freudian subconscious making it possible to take an interest in the inner life of the patient, since behind a disturbed consciousness he is not dissimilar to the doctor.

Secondly, schizophrenia invokes, paradoxically, a notion of wholeness in people's mental life: a split has taken place in an original whole. Psychiatry is conceptually, then, at odds with more general trends in the humanities. After modernism man *is* multifaceted, disunited and non-whole: the complex self which the novelist Knut Hamsun, whom we visit later in this chapter, described during his interviews with Dr Langfeldt, albeit without relation to schizophrenia, implicitly or explicitly. Hamsun felt a strong discomfort at the impenetrable wall between his own and his psychiatrist's "vision du monde". Is it possible that this most complex of psychiatric illnesses, schizophrenia, has received such a prominent position in psychiatry that its discursive paradigms have unintentionally influenced the rest of the field? It is somewhat puzzling that psychiatry continues to hold on to an image of a fractured or split whole which the rest of society no longer finds abnormal. Of course, the diagnosis of schizophrenia is a good deal more complex than this, but nonetheless this basic notion of the disease seems to have had a far wider influence than is generally realised.

Before immersing ourselves in the Gaustad material, we will take a moment to look at a hospital report which is taken from another psychiatric clinic, Vinderen. Famous in Norway, this report is both unique in its material base, but also has many things in common with the reports that make up the main body of our investigation.

THE PSYCHIATRIC FILE OF A LITERARY CELEBRITY

The Norwegian book-reading public became acquainted with a very unique psychiatric hospital report when Gabriel Langfeldt and Ørnulf Ødegaard published *Den rettspsykiatriske erklæring om Knut Hamsun* (1978) [The psychiatric judicial observation of Knut Hamsun] following the publication of Thorkild Hansen's *Prosessen mot Knut Hamsun* [The Proceedings against Knut Hamsun] (1978).[21] The octogenarian author, Knut Hamsun, was interned at

---

21 The arguments in this chapter largely follow an earlier article on the topic (Aaslestad, 1995).

a psychiatric clinic after the Second World War as a consequence of his active support for the Nazi occupying forces, in order to assess his mental state and level of accountability for his troublesome stance on Hitler's Germany. His hospital report illustrates the aforementioned insurmountable difference between the writer's and patient's perception of the patient's world. The report shows – as does so much of the material from Gaustad – an erratic mixture of warmth, indifference, stupidity and intelligence. In the following quote (from a psychological test during the judicial observation) it is evident that the patient's intellectual capacity is substantially higher than that of the writer. However, the hierarchy of the hospital is such that it will not disenfranchise the intellectually weakest; it is the lowest person in that hierarchy, Hamsun, who comes out the worst in the passage:

> Elementary school knowledge, such as the names of continents, and questions about who Luther, Napoleon, Bismarck were, were all satisfactorily answered. Likewise the number of citizens of Oslo and Norway. [. . .] However, he did poorly when explaining difference vs. similarity of two terms. For example, what is the difference between a child and a dwarf: Answer: Their ages. Difference between confidence and conceitedness: Conceitedness would lead you to losing your job after having gained it by confidence. (Langfeldt, Ødegaard, 1978, p. 92)

The author's last elegant and humorous aphorism is twisted into its opposite: an example of *not* knowing how to handle linguistic concepts.

Elementary school knowledge – once the symbol of all that was constant and reliable in society – is used intentionally in the material from Gaustad Hospital to test the patient's ability to orient himself. When viewed in retrospect, even such hard facts join the list of all things relative: a patient manages in 1947 "to translate some simple Latin into Norwegian", but fails on his equations and is described as showing signs of "mild autism, fairly severe hebephrenia, inappropriate affect" and of having "no awareness of his condition". Those of us no longer able to translate simple sentences from Latin would, of course, not be given such a diagnosis and the example shows how variable and fragile our common educational backgrounds are.

"He knows the significance of the Christian festivals, yet initially identifies the Easter lamb as the object of the Easter Holidays, Ascension as belonging to the Pentecost," a writer records resignedly of another patient in the 1920s. The shared common culture of Norwegians, which breaks through even the confused speech of the psychotic, is subject to change over time, and with a significant passage of time, things can become quite incomprehensible. One has a glimpse into the communication problems that might arise with patients from altogether different cultural backgrounds.

In the Gaustad notes, these factual tests are also used to maintain minimal intelligible verbal interaction. The following rather touching extract is an example of what Roman Jakobson calls the *phatic function* of language, in which the object of speech is to ensure one has contact, that is, that the physical channels for communication between two people are open (of the type "Hello?" – "Hello?").

The *referential* content of this next extract points backwards to antiquity:

> Sits with his back towards the room and warms himself at the radiator. Coughs, splutters and swallows in his usual way – [. . .] (2nd Punic War?) Smiles – "218–201 B.C.".

To me it seems that the "best" writers over the years display an understanding that the communication of referential content is just *one* of the many functions of language.

Returning to our author, Hamsun, we find a clear difference in *narrative attitude* between the notes of the two psychiatrists who worked on his case. Hamsun himself spoke well of Ødegaard in his biographical book *On Overgrown Paths*.

> There were two professionals, but one of them [Ødegaard] stayed – or was kept – almost entirely out of it. I visited the director twice, each time perhaps for a quarter of an hour, but he struck me as being a likable man without pretensions, with whom one could converse. (Hamsun, 1956, p. 270f; from the letter to the state attorney 23 July 1946)

Dr Ødegaard's notes in the report are indeed less voluminous compared to those of Langfeldt. But since Ødegaard was the director of Gaustad Hospital in the period 1938–71, we have access to many of his other notes in our chosen corpus and can recognise the unpretentious humanity with which Hamsun credits him. The quote below is taken from a record penned by Ødegaard, about one of his patients at Gaustad during the 1950s. Again it exemplifies the 'elementary school knowledge test' in its phatic function:

He completes the smaller multiplication table easily, 11 times 13 he suggests makes 131, and refuses to shift, but says instead that he will "happily write the sum out, if that's what you want." He is given a pencil and paper and draws up a very impressive piece of adding up which does indeed give the correct answer, but which the undersigned cannot fathom the principles of. *The last round therefore goes to the patient, on that note it is probably wisest to conclude the session.* [italics added]

The director describes the relationship between the patient and doctor using a humorous boxing metaphor, and seems to have no difficulty allowing the patient the last word. As readers we may be impressed by this warmth and understanding, yet, as we touched on in the section on Foucault above, the note's untroubled style is probably predicated on the same assumption of the writer's absolute authority. The quote below is taken from Dr Ødegaard's concluding summary after the assessment of Hamsun:

> *He rejects indignantly* [any suggestion] that there might be anything wrong with his faculties – that is what they want to make out; this must surely come from the State Prosecutor *he says*. The stay at the clinic is torture for him – going through three locked doors just to get outside in the air, and the same three locked doors back again (gestures impatiently with his hands the locking of each door) [. . .]
>
> When you speak loudly enough into his left ear for him to hear *he understands everything.* He is generally attentive and interested in our conversations, at times quite engaged – at other times he sits back in his chair and apparently falls into thought, but is easy to reengage. His language is clear and ordered, usually very precise in his expressions, *and full of Hamsunesque phrases.* He only rarely searches for words, and only occasionally will he use a wrong word, but then corrects himself immediately. (Langfeldt, Ødegaard, 1978, p. 76f, italics added)

This is a "well-written" note. It is clear who says what; the finite nexus of "he rejects" in the first line is made more immediate with the description of the tone of the patient's voice (*"indignantly"*). After the first dash, the text expresses opinions that turn out to be Hamsun's speech ("he says"). The next quote is not in quotation marks and is apparently direct speech, but the pronoun has shifted to the third person ("for him") which makes it into a form of free indirect speech. After the parenthetical insertion, which both describes and interprets a physical movement, follows a substantial evaluation of the communication situation.

In the italicised *"and full of Hamsunesque phrases"* the doctor lets his *own admiration of the author's language* come to the surface of the note. It is rare for such a liberty to be taken in our material. Is it fear of the subjective unscientificness that censures our writers from any sudden flashes of personal opinion?

The emphasised points in the extract below also signal the doctor's sympathy for patient's situation and position:

> Emotionally he is relaxed and measured. He is generally forthcoming – a little impatient at the necessity of going through all these questions again, but he immediately understands when told that personal impressions are important. He becomes agitated when the topic comes up of his being locked up, and especially over the psychiatric observation– *but no more than is wholly understandable* – he may raise his voice a little, and uses occasional strong expressions, e.g. that this is torture, but quickly calms down again (ibid, p. 77, italics added)

Dr Ødegaard's subjectivising notes invite the reader to see the report writer and the system he represents in a critical light at the same time as the observation is carried out: it is no wonder that Knut Hamsun grows agitated by being compulsorily admitted into a psychiatric clinic to undergo a mental examination. The writer does not make any moral capital out of his own ethical qualities or his understanding of the patient, which certainly manifest themselves as greater than that of his colleague. The writer's digressions are halted mid-flow, and he immediately pulls back and the statement is continued at the most syntactically appropriate place after a dash.

Langfeldt's text, on the other hand, does not contain any such *digressions* in which sympathy flows momentarily in the direction of the patient. In the extract below one can sense the narrow-minded scientist confronted with an author of enormous talent; doubtless the writer revealed more of himself in this note than he might ideally have liked:

> (Memory?) "I remember the very last days, of course." (11 × 12?) "Oh, I have never been good at sums, professor, once I calculated myself out of 5000 kroner, another time I calculated myself a gain of 1000 kroner. Even though

I worked as a shop assistant as a youngster." (7×9?) "63." (What did your parents die from?) (ibid, p. 57)

The layout of the note may seem respectful and fair; with the writer's speech put in parentheses, thus foregrounding the statements of the patient. However such a dialogue illustrates the writer's absolute control of the conversation. The interviewer *could* have at least paused momentarily at the three pieces of information offered by Hamsun that invite conversation (too much and too little money, and a childhood memory, all of which are touched on with humour and cheerfulness); if nothing else the doctor could have paused just to ensure the progress of communication, but instead he ploughs on posing multiplication questions, thus keeping rigidly to his aim, irrespective of any detours, demonstrating that he is not a man to be sidetracked. One might also detect a veiled threat in the gradual lowering of difficulty in the multiplication tables: *senility* surely lurks at some hidden lower limit. Where is the line drawn? Somewhere below the 5 times table perhaps? This repeated marking of distance to whatever the patient says, ensures, perhaps, that the writer is perceived as more scientific than others? Perhaps *turning a deaf ear* guarantees a scientific tenor, since it prevents the conversation from going off track?

Seen in its historical context, it may be that Langfeldt feels the need to demonstrate that his political sympathies are in the right place by *not* allowing himself be charmed by this linguistically seductive author, once adored by his nation, now reviled as a traitor. But it may be that even more trivial reasons lie behind Langfeldt's attitude. His lack of understanding of the author Hamsun has always puzzled me. Langfeldt's son has explained that his father *never* read novels. He only bought and ploughed through Hamsun's collected works when the task of the psychological examination was given to him in 1945.[22] In this light it seems easier to understand Langfeldt's often less than subtle remarks about Hamsun's writing. Reading novels is not a requirement of an intellectual, but it was much more so 50 years ago – and our subject was, after all, one of Norway's greatest novelists, a Nobel Prize winner with whose works most people should be familiar. The arrogance Hamsun accuses Langfeldt of seems even more glaring when viewed in the light of his son's information.

---

22 Interview with Knut M Langfeldt in the Norwegian newspaper *Arbeiderbladet*, 19 September 1996, by Turid Larsen.

An entry by a nurse (7/1/1946) reveals the system from the perspective of both patient and ward. If one has read the biographies of Hamsun's wife, Marie, it would be hard to free oneself from the image of a man suffering from excessive pedantry, but even with this knowledge at the back of one's mind, the reader of the entry below will probably – rather than spotting a pedant – sense a Kafkaesque abuse of power:

> Pt. very upset that his suitcase has been gone through and that his shirts are now on the shelf rather than in the suitcase. Unfortunately his razor blade sharpener has been used by the nurses for other patients and a damage has occurred; a cut in the strap. This is another thing he wants to hold the clinic responsible for. (ibid, p. 68f)

The anxiety over the dispersed ego, spread out over shelves and on the ward – is described by the unsuspecting writer in such a way that one recognises this contemporary man's feelings of diminishment when faced with such an institutionalised structure. An understanding made more acute, of course, when one knows that the patient in question is one of the founders of Modernism.

Eventually, all communications between Langfeldt and Hamsun take place in writing, as was the case in this attempt at arriving at a character analysis:

> Langfeldt: In the report I have to give to the authorities about you, I need to include a description of your character traits. It would be very useful to hear what you thought about these yourself – as I assume that in the course of your life you have analysed yourself thoroughly. As far as I can see, you have always been aggressive. Can you explain if you think that is something you were born with, or is it rooted in certain experiences in childhood?
>
> At the same time I have the impression that you are very sensitive – vulnerable. Is that correct? And what other character traits do you carry in you? Suspicious? Egotistical or generous? Have you a jealous nature? A highly developed sense of right and wrong? Logical? A sensitive or cold nature?
>
> Hamsun: I have not analysed myself in any other way than through the creation of hundreds of characters in my books – each spun from myself, with the shortcomings and strengths that fictitious people have. [. . .] I do not think that in all my work, from the moment I began, I have created a single person with this kind of straightforward governing attribute. They are

all without so-called 'character', they are split and fragmented, neither good nor bad, but both, nuanced, and changeable in mind and action. As I am, undoubtedly, myself.

It is perfectly possible that I am aggressive, that I may have a little of all the traits the Professor intimates – vulnerable, suspicious, egotistic, sensitive, jealous, a strong sense of right and wrong, logical, a cold nature; they would be human, all these characteristics. But I don't know if I can give priority to any one of them in myself.

What defines me, in addition to all the above, is the blessing that has enabled me to write my books. But I cannot 'analyse' that. Brandes called it 'divine Madness'. (ibid, p. 82f)

Here, we see a fundamental conflict between the professor's *naturalistic* worldview and the writer's *modernistic* outlook; the one view sees people as being defined by a single, overriding characteristic, while the other sees people as subject to a shifting conglomerate of characteristics. Hamsun expresses himself explicitly on this topic:

The so-called naturalistic period, Zola and his time, wrote about people with dominant character traits. They had no use of more nuanced psychology, for them people had "governing" characteristics that guided their actions.

Dostoyevsky and others taught us all something different about people. (ibid)

In many ways it seems that Langfeldt – in direct line from *Zola* – has been decisive for the aesthetics of the descriptive fragments in the Gaustad records all the way to the present day. Descriptions like: "As a child he was bright and cheerful", which I would normally associate with the romantic peasant novels of mid-nineteenth century Norway, appear in the standard repertoire of the psychiatric record surprisingly recently. These are written by people who seem to have received their literary education within a system that has still failed to adopt a (more Ibsenesque) scepticism towards the ability of language to capture and embrace a unified and coherent world.

Hamsun would exact a cruel revenge on Langfeldt when he published *On Overgrown Paths* in 1949, a book about his stay in Vinderen Psychiatric Clinic. When Ødegaard and Langfeldt published their court psychiatric report in 1978, it must have been with an eye to providing a more nuanced picture of the author's stay in the hospital. Yet the undeniable literary quality of Hamsun's book had already resulted in the public seeing, as Hamsun had intended, that the hospital's diagnosis of "permanent mental impairment" was wholly unfounded.

In *On Overgrown Paths* it was the *patient* who offered the reader a picture of his doctor:

> I feel that he [Professor Langfeldt] is the type of seminarist who has come back from the seminary with all the bookish knowledge he has gathered from school books and learned works, and which he has naturally kept himself up to date with through continued study. [. . .] He is so sure in his knowledge. But that is not the same as being sure in the old wisdom: certain only that nothing is certain. In his personality, in his way of being, Mr. Langfeldt sets himself way above everybody with his uncontestable learning, with his silence at any disagreement, with his show of superiority which seems merely contrived. [. . .] I feel the psychiatrist would benefit from learning how to smile a little. *A smile directed at himself now and then*. (Hamsun, 1956, p. 292f, italics added)

What we can now sadly see in retrospect, after the publication of the psychiatric records in 1978, is that Hamsun was right. Langfeldt – even in the briefest of fragments – reveals Hamsun's description to be accurate, as we saw in the example of the multiplication questions.

Focus in recent years on lobotomy procedures has meant that Ødegaard is now seen as the psychiatric abuser. But of the two psychiatrists, he was the only one capable of smiling with self-mocking and camaraderie – a smile that might have given Hamsun some confidence in, and respect for, psychiatry.

As a reader, I find it difficult not to identify with, and to enter into the role of the patient, particularly when he is clearly not insane and when he bears the name Knut Hamsun. Hamsun's discussion with Langfeldt shows, amongst many things, how difficult it has been for psychiatry to adopt twentieth century modernism. Is it generally the case that current ideas that might have entered almost all other forms of writing in the present day, do *not* get represented in hospital records? That, as Kristeva suggests, the hospital is so entrenched in its symbolic position that absolutely nothing will shift it? When is an "ideational current" so integral to our worldview that a piece of writing revealing a lack of knowledge of it, loses its currency?

And is it the case that psychiatric hospital records will forever reflect a style of writing that is passé elsewhere?

Is the psychiatric record subliminally obliged to maintain a more conservative text ideology, in line with the founding principles of the asylum, keeping a distance from the patient and his immediate environment?

3

First period: 1890–1920

THE PROTOCOL

The oldest records in our corpus are written in large, leather-bound year-books for the men's and women's wards, and arranged according to passage of time and the organisation of the hospital. Each volume has one page per patient. At the top of each page we find the patient's name, age, occupation, possible hereditary factors, diagnosis and the presumed cause of illness. At the front of the book there is an alphabetical register of names, and at the back are the regulations of King Oscar II on the running of asylums. Each yearbook begins with the patient that has been in the hospital the long-est, and proceeds chronologically according to admission dates. The latest arrival therefore gets the first blank page. The year's steady progression is the external chronology that determines the structure of the book. After the last admission, with the arrival of the New Year, a new book is begun.

There is a gradual tendency for the notes for each patient to get longer. One page is not always enough; in these cases the notes continue on the first available page at the end. If this second page also proves insufficient, the notes continue further back; a reader must therefore leaf back and forth through the volume to follow the patient's record; the books grow increas-ingly unwieldy, the physical form ruptures from within, and eventually individual folders arrive as a replacement. The system cannot hold the unified yearly accounts and moves instead to individualised records around 1920.

Later, the record folders seem to suffer the same fate as the old leather-bound casebooks; they bulge, becoming less and less tidy, receiving steadily more addendums from a growing number of authorities. The same informa-tion is repeated over and over again.

THE LAW

Placed inside the cover of these huge, leather-bound casebooks was a copy of
"Law on the Treatment and Care of the Mentally Insane" in which Paragraph
5 is dedicated the writing of records:[23]

> In every asylum for the insane a Personnel Protocol and Treatment Protocol
> shall be kept. In the former, wherein a copy of the present regulations shall
> be inserted, will be recorded on admission the Name, Age, Place of Birth,
> Occupation and Residence of every patient, as well as the name of the per-
> son at whose request the Patient is to be admitted to the Asylum. Within a
> period of 8 days after admission a comprehensive description of the Patient's
> Physical and Mental condition and any subsequent changes that may occur,
> must be recorded in this protocol.

Thus, it is the letter of the Law that forms the starting point for these
casebooks; the law is a basis for medical practice. The formal status of the
psychiatric record is emphasised *before* the writing begins. The writing, by
order of Royal decree, is something *more* than the book in which it is entered.
The unusual height and thickness, and the leather spine with gold lettering
detailing the name of the asylum and the year, signals that it is a worthy text
the reader is about to embark upon.

The notes – however varied they may be – constitute a part, then as now,
of the fulfilment of legal regulations, and strive to satisfy any requirements
these (e.g. the Mental Health Act) might require. The official appearance of
the protocol, and its association with royalty, ensure that these records and
their writing face *outwards* towards the wider context of society's institutions:
no matter how closed the asylum may seem to the patient, the hospital is
not alone in managing the individual patient's story.

The records from Gaustad Hospital's first period do not differ essentially
from those produced 100 years later. The 1890 records start, just as the later
ones, with a transcript of a note from the admitting doctor. This is then
followed by "The comprehensive description of the Patient's Physical and
Mental condition" which according to the law must be entered a few days
later, as a Status Praesens. Then follow some sporadic, short notes intended
to record any observed changes in the patient's condition, initially in

---

23 The law is dated Malmø, 17 August 1848, published in Christiania, printed at
  Grøndahl.

contrast to the patient's condition on admission, and then later in contrast to any preceding notes.

THE STATIC. FREQUENCY

Content-wise, there is a focus in these short notes on the patient's *physical behaviour*. Notes describing any change in behaviour patterns end with a brief conclusion concerning a move to another ward; *down* the alphabet for deteriorating behaviour, *upwards* for improvements; the latter being afforded fewer and shorter notes, proving Montgomery Hunter correct, it seems, in her observation that; "Where success is expected it is not a criterion of narratability" (*see* above p. 29).

Our textual commentary will, in the main, deal with the report's micro level, and will concern itself in particular with the relationship between Discourse (the running text) and the Story (the reality referred to). In this context the notion of so-called *frequency* is particularly relevant in the study of hospital notes. Frequency within narratology concerns itself with repetition. Normally we imagine that we relate something *once* that happened *once*, a so-called singulative narrative. However, we also find descriptions that highlight what *usually* happens: for example, "*Every* evening I went to bed early,"[24] the so-called iterative narrative, which narrates something *once* that happened *n* times in the story. It is very common for a narrative to begin iteratively, and then move into a singulative mode, that is, we first learn what usually happens, then we are told about a single event, ". . . *but* yesterday I went to bed late." This is a common tradition in the novel; against a background of something that constantly repeats itself (the iterative), something unique takes place (singulative), which is worth telling. Logically we can also imagine the other two possibilities of repetition; the telling *n* times what happened *n* times in the story, "I went to bed early yesterday, I went to bed early the day before etc. . . .", so-called anaphoric frequency. This form may seem hypothetical, but we see it regularly in the writing of notes and diaries. The narrator cannot see into the future and cannot therefore offer any introductory, summarising "every day". To relate *n* times that which

---

24 The example of going to bed early is Genette's playful rewrite of the opening to Marcel Proust's *In Search of Lost Time*. Genette's *Narrative Discourse*, which is the English translation of his *Discours du récit*, is, as opposed to what many believe, not so much a text book on narratology as an analysis of Proust's great novel.

happened *once* in the story, so-called *repeating narrative*, may seem even more hypothetical but the form is found in various modernist texts, if the aim for example is to mimic obsessive speech or emphasise fanatic attention to one single occurrence.

By focusing on the manifestation of frequency in notes, and reflecting on the relationships and distribution of, especially singulative, iterative and anaphoric frequency, we have a tool to expose some of the underlying perceptions of reality which the records do not formulate explicitly.

Returning to the 1890s: gradual improvement is, as we mentioned above, given scant attention in notes. On the other hand we find a large number of notes that document deterioration, along the lines of the following:

> 1 (1890) Been calm and agreeable for some time, but more disagreeable of late, slams the door, throws cups, and throws stones in the yard. To C.[25]

The non-finite "for some time" is contrasted with the "of late". Both extremes in the note are governed by repetition, the iterative. Fragments, such as this, in which an unusual event happens, generally begin with a description of how things are usually (iterative frequency), before we are informed about what is peculiar in this instance (singulatively). Despite the fact that the fragment describes, as required by law, a transitional description, between the way things have been "for some time" and what has happened "of late" – what comes through is an extreme sense of a fundamentally static, or unchanging situation. The break that comes with "of late" is deceptive. The new information is *also* non-finite in time: "slams the door, throws cups, and throws stones in the yard." For how long has this been happening? Is this the Dantean, eternal static inferno that is being realised here? In Dante's inferno, Man is locked into his most prominent characteristics, doomed to eternal repetition, without any possibility of looking towards the future or any change.

The writer of this note from the 1890s consistently expresses himself through so-called sentence fragments,[26] the grammatical subject is removed. From the protocol we know that the extract above concerns a woman – but

---

25 The entries are copied in their original form. Misspellings are corrected but linguistic peculiarities maintained.

26 Sentence fragments are phrases where we feel the lack of a subject or the finite verb (in present or past tense), without any significant change to the semantic content of the phrase.

the writer finds it unnecessary to report other aspects of the person than those that occasion a move to a ward with worse patients. The end of the fragment, "To C", reveals nothing of the expectations or projections of future events. There is a "silent" conclusion. Her insanity – too serious for Ward B – will not deviate from the norm on Ward C, and the silence surrounding the patient will be reinstated once more.

In the following fragment too, this same static, unchanging quality is reflected in the surprising use of the present tense:

> 2 (1890) Unsettled last night, disturbing others, is utterly confused, complains about this damned matron coming and going every day. To D.

The note, we have to assume, is authored in retrospect, when the move to D has been decided, but is written as if the night is everlasting. It is rare for such short notes to give glimpses of the verbal remarks of the patients. The writer here is communicating the conclusion first, "utterly confused", followed by a relatively every-day phrase, which is offered as an example of the insane patient's speech. So self-evident is this patient's place in the hierarchy – always somewhere between C and D – that it makes no difference whether the writer turns the causal relationship upside-down and gives his evaluation first, followed by his observation.

This next example also goes, despite its temporal adverbial "in the last few days", in the direction of something static, although a little more subtly than in previous examples.

> 3 (1890) The last few days more than usually hostile with loud screeching voice. To D for today.

Both the grammatical subject and the finite verb ("she is . . .") have been left out. The focus is on the *screeching voice*, which seems somehow detached from the person. As such the note is impressionistic – it is the noise alone which is communicated, the noise as it dominates the ward. She is always screeching, but the last few days more so than usual – this added description of the patient's "screeching" may indicate that a threshold of irritation has been crossed. Does moving her represent a form of treatment? Is there an expectation that the poorer conditions of Ward D will drive her back to the her usual level of screeching, or is it Ward C that needs a break from the noise? The *noise* has gained prominence over the *person*. The wards and asylum appear solid and unchallengeable – as do the collected protocols – while the patients' voices dissolve polyphonically within their walls. "Difficult and obstinate. To Ward D in thick blankets" represents a standard pattern; subject-less and verb-less, it renders the patient identity-less on the ward.

THE INTENTION OF THE ASYLUM

The focus on physical behaviour was, as we have seen, insisted on by the law that required the recording of all changes in the condition of patients. More than once, during the reading of the oldest records I puzzled over how few of the patients' thought processes were communicated. We have already seen how a relatively everyday sentence, about the "damned matron" was presented as an example of confused speech; the writer had no need to contextualise the phrase to explain the "utter confusion" of the patient. Here we can discern how the text refuses, at all costs, to let go of a symbolic order, and how it keeps the semiotic pressure under control, much in line with Kristeva's thinking (*see* above p. 26).

A more historically rooted explanation for the absence of madness in these texts, can be found in the hospital's understanding of itself. From the earliest days one of the main premises for treatment in Gaustad Hospital was that the professionals would *not* enter into the imaginative world of the mental patient. In a publication marking Gaustad's fifteenth year (1871), the hospital's then director, O. Sandberg, wrote:

> As long as the Illness is at its peak, any Counterargument, every tangible Proof, will be wasted; but gradually – and this is a good sign – the Patient will start little by little to listen to Counterarguments and express a tentative Doubt as to the truth of their Delusions, allowing attempts to [work on them]; however, only on a couple of Occasions have I succeeded in achieving anything by direct Counterargument [. . .] (Sandberg, 1871, p. 116, footnote)

This attitude towards treatment is reflected in the records, in their comprehensive discretion in relation to the distorted world of the patient. This goes for most of the 100-year period. Patients' delusions may sometimes be catalogued in the record, but it is rare for them to leave any traces in the shape of retrospective commentary about their content. Exceptions are found in the 1920s, where a seemingly equal dialogue between doctor and patient is recorded in the notes, and again in the 1970s, where the notes often contain analytical evaluations of the delusions.

In the same 1871 publication, which was aimed at the country's medical profession, Sandberg gives an account of what he calls "the psychological treatment". The patient must, from the outset of his treatment, have *calm*, and be safely distanced from his usual environment. After a while he may participate in distracting work and leisure activities, and later there may be opportunities for visits from home:

> On the condition that the Illness has reached such a Level, that the Admission is justified, the Admission itself forms one of the greatest psychological Measures, and one must not let oneself be swayed by these vulgar Arguments that a person will of course become insane if they are put with the Insane etc. I would implore my Colleagues not to let themselves be *assuaged* by such Talk. No! If the Admission is needed, then one should not take it lightly, for it is through the Admission itself that the most important Causal Indication is fulfilled, *as the Patient is torn away from the Family Relationships, those Arguments, Annoyances, Sorrows and Worries, that have made the Home into the Hearth of the illness; yes, from the very Places, Surroundings and People which due to the Patient's Moods and Irrational Ideas have become his worst Torment, it is good for him to be removed,* and not only is the Causal Indication fulfilled by the Cutting off of these sources of his illness, but when the Conditions in the Asylum are not, through Overcrowding or other Irregularities, too unfavourable, *then the patient will find there a serviceable – Asylum.* The calmness and order of it will, in some way, contrast with the Troubles and Worries of the Home [. . .] Generally, by doing nothing else and solely by removing Contact with these, and by encouraging other Ideas, a favourable psychological distraction will be created – and in order to provide this, every Asylum must have, as Gaustad has, the Provision of useful Employment, which without strain provides Material requiring Attention and Reflection, for Education in School Subjects, Music etc, as well as in Handicrafts, Agriculture and Gardening, in order to offer Amusement and finally for Religious Instruction, Character building and Comfort. (ibid, p. 115ff, italics added)

This distance to the *illness* of the patient may also be observed in the patient notes as a fundamental attitude – although not always with such benign reserve as in the director's summary. The illness should be as invisible as possible, and be logged in the records only when it breaks too much with the established norms of the ward. In Kristeva's terminology: the semiotic pressure is constantly held at bay. This reveals an understandable desire to keep the universe of the hospital as ordered as possible – at the same time it also hints at the highly charged emotions that are pent up beneath this well-ordered writing.

SILENCE AS NEGLECT

It is difficult not to be affected by *the empty pages* in the records up to 1920. In the later folders one has to look carefully at the dates of the entries to see if an inordinately long time has passed since last time the patient was *found worthy of any remark*. But in the leather-bound casebooks, in which every person is initially afforded a whole page which is then filled according to need, silence manifests itself clearly in the form of empty pages. Curiosity grows too, when one sees the same person appearing in successive yearly volumes, logged by number, name, age, profession, cause of illness and diagnosis, but never a single word more. For instance, throughout the 1890s there is complete silence about a patient on the Women's Ward, who occupies the first page of every single casebook. Her name, age, occupation (daughter of farmer), admission date (1869), diagnosis and the presumed cause of her illness are reported identically each year. What, one wonders, lies hidden behind these empty pages? Then, in 1897 something finally happens, more than the superficial change of "probable cause of illness" from "onanism" to "masturbation". On the 9 December the silence is broken when, in a one-line entry, the patient is described as "reportedly upset and less unclean". And then in the week that follows we read:

> 4 (1897) her condition is unchanged, she speaks nonsense, often rudely yelling (e.g. called the doctor "you bastard", kicked after him when he greeted her), moves her hands as if sewing or playing piano, regularly talking in the night, steadily "less unclean".

As a reader the excitement at eventually finding a more detailed description of this patient is so great, that one feels drawn into *her* situation. But does the comment about her unchanged behaviour refer to the last week – or *the last 30 years of silence*? If her textual silence reflects the institution's neglect of her, it is quite a thrill to learn about her kicking out at the doctor (a reaction at last!), a reaction completely at odds, of course, to the writer's intention. For the writer is meticulous in his task, required as he is by the law to record precisely any *changes in the patients' condition*. (the use of narrative frequency is commented on in the chapter on hierarchies (*see* p. 58).

As a reader, 100 years on, I experience the text from the opposite angle to the writer. My compassion reaches out to the person who, for 30 years, has been given no consideration other than to be counted as present. Yet such righteous indignation cannot be directed wholly at the writer, who is fulfilling his job within a given framework.

A glance at some of the historical context surrounding this patient file, may temper the despondency of the reader. There is scant evidence to challenge our general impression of the nineteenth century's asylums as mere depositories for people, but to gain a wider perspective of the hospital treatment we must look at how Gaustad's director, Sandberg, depicts conditions *outside* the hospital walls.

TREATMENT OUTSIDE THE HOSPITAL

From the start, Gaustad was one of the most modern and well-respected hospitals in Europe. In the publication marking Gaustad's first 15 years, Dr Sandberg shared some of his own experiences of the kinds of treatment which the insane might experience outside the hospital environment. It must have made harrowing reading, even for the district doctors of 1870, for whom this book was intended. The following example illustrates both the inability of a patient's home village to look after the insane, and the superiority of the hospital's treatment:

> On the occasions he tore himself loose, the Neighbourhood would rush in, as if an Accident had taken place, and catch him with a rope; for there is Nobody who personally dares bind him. In the last 6 months this Man has been resident at Gaustad, where he arrived bound and tied. Excepting some passing bad moods, he has, throughout the entire Time here, shown himself to be polite and agreeable, and a very hard working and skilled Worker; his behaviour has never given rise to any use of force or incarceration. (Sandberg, 1871, p. 288)

Sandberg describes the tying up of the insane that he has witnessed in villages, but goes on to say that it is "not the Chain itself that is the worst [aspect] of their treatment at home": he gives a number of examples of people who live under the most inhumane conditions, of which we include one:

> When I saw him on my Travels, he had been locked up for about 4 years. On a cold Winter's day he was to be found a small Room in an Outhouse, dressed in a Shirt. At one Wall was a frightfully hot wood burner, which was fed from outside [. . .] In the door, which was rarely opened, was a hatch, through which his food was passed. The Vessels which contained the Food often came back filled with his Excrement, as he seemed to find pleasure in the disgust that this created in those tending him. There was a small Hatch in the Floor for the Removal of Excrement, but he amused himself more by throwing it around and soiled everything he could get hold of. In Relationship to me he was quite amenable, he complained that they wanted to kill him with Fire and Smoke, but otherwise spoke quite confusedly. His family wanted him admitted to Gaustad for a time, where he is now. He is in a very confused state, and has seemed rather threatening on a couple of occasions – but he is always decently dressed, lives and sleeps with the other patients, and has even participated usefully in wood cutting. He is usually content and cheerful. His family now find themselves unable to pay for his keep anymore [. . .] he will therefore possibly soon have to return, and be submitted yet again to his previous treatment. (ibid, p. 287f)

In both these "case stories" we notice Sandberg's pride in the treatment Gaustad offers. Sandberg reminds his readers that all the way up to his own century the asylums have been largely geared towards protecting society *against* the mad. But in his institution another, more important element has been added:

> The purpose of the care needs to be 1) to make their existence as good as possible, and 2) to make them as harmless as possible. (ibid, p. 285f)

Using treatment without coercion in the asylums, the sick can become "not only harmless, but even useful and hardworking". (ibid, p. 286) This is in essence what the hospital strives for, and it would be surprising if this very sympathetic ethos should not also be evidenced in its reports. But we have already seen in Amalie Skrams's novel *Professor Hieronimus* how this ethos of usefulness and industry could be as repellent as it was positive (*see* p. 16). We will also see examples of understandable resistance to ideas regarded by the contemporary majority as having positive value. One of the challenges the writer undoubtedly faces is to understand the significance of this opposition and find a place for it in his notes.

SILENCE AS TREATMENT

During the initial period following the patient's admission there should, according to Sandberg, be "calm" – and beyond this "nothing should be done".

Silence in these texts is therefore not blameworthy; on the contrary, from the perspective of the writer's naïve or confident position, it contributes to the fulfilment of the purpose of the asylum. Yet to the reader, 100 years later, the purposefully constructed and well-intentioned silence of these notes, looks, at some point, like culpable neglect. "For it is all very fine to keep silence, but one has also to consider the kind of silence one keeps," as the protagonist in Samuel Beckett's *The Unnameable* says. Even if the writer has both the law and the asylum's humane and forward-looking intentions on his side – yet when this silence is maintained for 30 years, one cannot help feeling some anger as a reader; such a period surely displays a lack of proportion on the part of the writer.

This silence can, however, be justified if it is assumed that "the patient is contented here". The absence of a bad conscience in the narrative text – so unlike that of our own time – is understandable in a historic context when, for example, we look at Sandberg's shocking, even, agitational depiction of care within the family or local community, as an inhuman alternative. But one should not loose sight of the fact that care of the insane within their families and communities was a topic heavily debated around the turn of the nineteenth century, and conclusions were very ambiguous.[27]

---

27 For the sake of curiosity as well as balance, let me quote from the district physician Dr Østvold who was of the opposite persuasion. The following extract is taken from his article "Om privatforpleining af sindssyge [On the private care of the insane]" which appeared in *Tidsskrift for Praktisk Medicin [Journal of Practical Medicine]* (1899, pp. 205–10): "Because it has happened, that people discharged from asylums as incurably insane have become quite normal, and it is not uncommon to find considerable improvement following good private care [at home or in the community]. In those where there is still some spirit left, it seems reasonable to assume that life in familiar surroundings, amongst the people from whom they were separated, should prove gainful, once the more serious conditions requiring treatment at an asylum have subsided" (p. 207). Again, we note how the same phenomenon can receive the opposite interpretation.

THE HIERARCHY

Let us return for a moment, to the linguistic form of the 1890 fragment (No 4); the women who calls the doctor "a bastard". Once more the fragment insists on the static, unchanging quality of the situation, through the use of the present tense and iterative frequency. A present participle (yelling) is also used and contributes significantly to the sense of recurrence. The patient's kicking out at the doctor is, however, a one-time event, which thus stands out in even stronger relief against this static universe. The writer points to the patient's insolence towards the doctor as the prime example of her hostile behaviour, yet leaves it uncommented on and discreetly placed in parentheses. This is not the last time we find an attack on somebody high in the hospital hierarchy depicted as particularly reprehensible behaviour on the part of a patient. The following note is representative:

> 5 (1899) Extremely rude and challenging. Argumentative at table so that one pt. had to leave the table, and also towards the director.

The rudeness that the *wardens* presumably endure on a daily basis goes unrecorded. There are clear dividing lines in the hospital hierarchy between the director and the doctors on the *visible* side, and everyone else on the *invisible* side. The writers from the wards are also included in this silent majority. They are invisible *and silent about their own writing* as they write. The writer of the 1890s never leaves a trace of his own writing activity. This is in stark contrast to the writers of the present day, who do not shy away from appropriating the text for themselves, and consequently away from the patient, who should, of course, be at the centre. The following extract from 1985 illustrates this contrast:

> 6 (1985) He almost bullies his way into staying and says we have to call the police to evict him. *It was the end of the day, those of us who were involved wanted to go home and after vigorous discussion one decided to offer him an emergency bed until the morning* [. . .] [italics added]

The note-writer presents his own understanding of the situation; not in relationship to the patient, but to the *workplace* and to the working situation ("the end of the day", i.e. the end of the *shift*). Simultaneously, the voice of a kind of undefined collective body speaks here – somewhere between first and third person plural: ". . . those of us who were involved." The writer does not use "I" or even "we" but *those of us*, in other words, the writer points to others being outside the situation; these others have nothing to do with what is happening and have, therefore, been free to leave. "We" act, but with some of us on the outside. "One" that is, nobody in particular, makes a decision that the patient be allowed to stay the night: But is "one" part of "those of us", or does he belong to "the others"? The "we" is not only divided, but our actions are dual, we want one thing and at the same time we want the opposite. But whatever the case, the decision is beyond reproach, since it is taken "after vigorous discussion" and by a "sender" who remains obscured and undefined.

The contrast between the narrator's *strong presence* in contemporary reports and his *absence* 100 years ago cannot be merely put down to conditions in the field of psychiatry. In the 1890s it *was* far more uncommon to reflect on one's own writing, or on what cognitive and emotional stirrings might underpin the final text. This is equally applicable to the novel of the time. Thus, much of the calmness and natural authority exuded by the oldest records, may also be related to such time-bound writing traditions.

Example 4, about the woman who calls the doctor a bastard, does not end with the singulative event (kicking out at the doctor), but ends calmly in an iterative image; "steadily less unclean". Placed in the present tense, it is not fixed in time, and the event of the patient's kicking out is not contextualised in either past or future. Perhaps she has been sitting like this – her hands playing piano in the air – throughout the silence of the 1890s? The writer concludes this entry with a brief reference to an earlier note (*"steadily* less unclean") in which the iterative is allowed to dominate, and, in so doing, removes himself from the story by placing himself within the internal writing system already in place: his note is decided by the content of a preceding one, as is his comment "unchanged" in the first line, which refers back to the previous week's log. The iterative picture of a patient who is "steadily less unclean" stands alone, however, independent of any context. Despite its bland meaninglessness, this picture, which is used by many writers in the Status Praesens, seems, for today's reader, to gain significance in the context of the silence which otherwise surrounds the patient.

THE LAST WORD

The end of a fragment often stays in the memory, particularly when the last lines point not only back to the immediate content of the text, but outwards towards something *else* which remains uncommented upon. These two possibilities – an "introvert" conclusion or an extrovert one that points towards something which has, until now, been undefined – can, once more, have quite different effects if it is the writer or patient have the final say. One has to admire those writers, who do *not* feel it necessary to take the last word for themselves; those who are generous enough to resist the chance to round the narrative off with "their version" of events:

> 7 (1901) Has got out of bed in the last few days and become very active at work, conscientious. She giggles at the question as to whether she still feels like a block of wood, and answers no. However, no awareness of illness. People had believed she was ill, but she had only come away from God, which she is still, but that doesn't mean she has to spend the whole day in bed being bored.

The narrative content of this fragment is kept within the horizon of the patient, in free indirect speech, but uses alternating tenses.[28] The narrative distance is indicated by the phrase "However, no awareness of illness"; this is sufficient for the narrator, who does not reveal any attitude in the text towards the contents of the patient's final statement.

It is rare that a patient is given the last word, and it virtually never happens in direct speech; this might well imply that the patient was in control of the asylum situation and worse, from the asylum's point of view, blur the hierarchical relationships. Yet, paradoxically, it has to be admitted that the patient having the last word can indicate that the system is relaxed about the doctor's absolute authority, as Foucault claims is characteristic of the asylums in the nineteenth century (*see* p. 15), and as we observed in the example of Ødegaard conceding "the last round to the patient" (*see* p. 38). The conclusion to these contradictory claims must be that the voice in the final part of the fragment necessarily carries added significance, but that the narratological analysis of this must engage with its historical context.

---

28 This, of course, predicates an acceptance that free indirect style can be manifested in such relatively short fragments as this.

The way in which patients exit these early records is highly stylised. It is rare for discharge notes in this first period to exceed two lines. Concluding formulations are uniform: "discharged cured"/"discharged recovered"/"discharged improved"/"discharged uncured"/"discharged dead". Such formulations mark that the conclusion of the narrative is final, in contrast to more contemporary follow-up notes which include information from "outpatient notes" and from outside the hospital. These create a stronger sense of the patient as an individual, and soften the boundaries between the hospital and the outside world. But they can also hide some unpleasant facts – for example, the suicide of a patient who has been discharged too soon, and whose death is not acknowledged in any visible way (more of this later).

The following discharge note, however, is representative of notes from our first period:

> 8 (1891) [. . .] has for some time remained stable and well-behaved; participated diligently and with interest in several domestic activities. Discharged cured.

The rationale for the conclusion "discharged cured" is often the patient's "good-behaviour" and "diligence" as in the example above. Today's reader may be puzzled by the emphasis on what, for us, seem rather moral precepts; but as we have seen in Sandberg's writing, the primary aim with treatment was to get people in employment.

Yet it takes only the simplest variations to make a standard report, like the one just quoted, into a short, stylised portrait-sketch:

> 9 (1897) (Ex servant girl, now pauper, 59) Has for some time been calm and well-behaved, a little scatty by nature, always busy, highly strung. She has worked diligently in the kitchen. Shows good awareness of illness. Discharged improved.

Between the patient remaining calm and "well behaved" on the one side, and "diligent" on the other, the writer also takes the liberty of adding a few characteristics "scatty", "highly strung" and "always busy", based, no doubt, on the impression she has made in the hospital's shared spaces. These characteristics are still neither time- or space-related. This little portrait is drawn in passing, impressionistically, while still not being anchored in any particular moment. This is the way she *is*. The writer has made his notes with unquestioned authority; there is no doubt expressed in his statements. Additionally the writer has himself included three modifiers; "a little", "always very", "easily", emphasising his nuanced approach.

The writer can also vary the formulations at the end of a patient record, by including the conventions of the patient's leave taking. The way a parting takes place may momentarily shake the hierarchy of patient and hospital. Even if the former subjugates him – or herself in this social act, it is nonetheless a *joint action*:

> 10 (1897) 65 years, crofter's wife. Remains unchanged, often abusive and angry, indecent in her speech, is at departure pleasant, happy and *smiling, and curtsies when bidding her farewells.* Discharged unchanged. [italics added]

The final description of the patient as she leaves, before the usual "discharged" formula, is immaterial to the report. Yet the writer allows the patient, despite her continuing madness, to contribute a wordless message with formal elegance. Instead of being allowed to disappear from the patient files "abusive and angry", she exits with a curtsy and a smile. The parting of patient and institution is given dignity. The hospital pays homage to itself in the note – the patient bows to the hospital in grateful reverence.

It is not unusual for a record to end with the patient giving the hospital a favourable testimonial. In the fragment below the hospital's function as asylum is highlighted:

> 11 (1899) When his departure is finalised, he thinks really that "he had a good time here and wouldn't have the same comfort from now on", W. gives an impression of wanting to stay and is somewhat moved at departure time, "thinks it is strange to be leaving this place".

The patient's comment can be seen as an unequivocal support of Sandberg's assertions as to the advantages of the asylum over care in the local community.

THE VOICE OF THE PATIENT

In the previous example we notice one of the most stylistically peculiar characteristics about the genre of the psychiatric report; the *pseudo-reporting of direct speech.* The quotation marks indicate that "the patient speaks now". At the same time there is *no change* in pronoun. The third person pronoun is kept, as if what we have is indirect speech: ". . . he had a good time here and wouldn't have the same comfort from now on." We could imagine that the words: "He said that . . ." are crossed out. It seems that something extraordinary is needed for the patient is allowed to utter the word "*I*" in a record. This grammatical peculiarity seems prevalent throughout the entire 100-year period of our research.

Not even in the longest Status Praesens notes, filling a whole page, is the use of "I" common when speech is recorded. The following example from 1898 is an exception:

> 12 (1898) Stat. Præ.: [. . .] His own perspective on his admission and his relation-ship to society is explained by him in an anecdote about a man over at B [Ward]., who said: "I believed the world was mad, the world believed I was mad, in the end they were too many for me." Apart from his behaviour on the day of admission he has been calm, cooperative, sensible and polite, with a slightly ironic smile: "It is irrelevant what I say; you all think I am mad anyway," he sometimes says when attempts are made to come closer to him.

Yet even in this example, the power of the word "I" is lessened. Firstly, in the anecdote about the "man over at B" the "I" does not refer to any of the parties involved in the exchange between patient and doctor. In the second case where the word "I" is used, it is a single utterance, given with the first person pronoun, but the writer's remark that follows the quote – "he sometimes says" – highlights it as an iterative expression, and thereby only a token of many identical occurrences. This is a very peculiar form of direct speech. Indeed, Marcel Proust achieved fame for its use in his novel *In Search of Lost Time*, although the Norwegian novelist Jonas Lie had already established a similar technique, allowing an apparently single phrase turn out to be an example of several identical ones. Interestingly, we have once again found stylistic characteristics of the novel occurring in our hospital records. Aesthetic characteristics, it would seem, have a value in types of writing other than literary prose.

The peculiar pronoun shifts from third to first person, which, contrary to expectation, we find frequently in our material, may be an indication of something as banal as the writer's unsteady concentration or insufficient ability to capture the situation linguistically. But read from the "hermeneutics of suspicion" governing this project, this linguistic peculiarity may also indicate a fear of using the word "I"; a fear of entering a situation from the *other person's* perspective, of becoming like *the other*, in the act of writing. This is not an unreasonable interpretation when one thinks how important it seems for the writer to have full control over the development of the text, and considering the huge pressure of madness that the writing has to withstand.

The following short note gives us a glimpse into the thought processes of the patient, while her actions are simultaneously linked to what she says. The missing use of first person pronoun, where one would formally expect it, possibly indicates an unresolved closeness-distance relationship between the writer and patient, *or* a narrative technical problem that is not easily resolvable within standard prose:

> 13 (1897) Sometimes she leaves her bed and lies on the floor, because she feels living animals in the sea grass – snakes and lizards – occasionally they have stung her pretty badly. She dismisses this as nonsense; however, she maintains that what "is connected to father, is not her father, because he is dead." Is quite vain and over-excitable. She hears voices in the night that say that she will be burned up; sometimes she also sees flames licking round her; laughs as she relates this. She went to bed for a few days, because she felt her head would break apart when they were talking in the workroom on B [Ward]. There were "echoes inside her head".

It is difficult to decide whether the first part of the first sentence is plain narrative text or the reporting of her speech without attribution. After the first comma we have an explanation of her behaviour (i.e. "because she feels living animals") motivated by her previous experiences. Starting with the description of "living animals in the sea grass", it is the patient's vocabulary that flavours the text. Her voice shines through that of the writer, and, to return to Bakhtin, her linguistic zone spreads out over the narrative text (*see* p. 33). The writer intervenes, in the next remark, with meta-commentary concerning the patient's own attitude to what she has said, confirming that she herself takes distance to it. Midway through the note the telling of her story is interrupted by the writer's description of her. Here the writer does not relate to *the content of what she is saying* but to her as a *person* ("quite vain and over-excitable"); again we note the omission of subject and verb. What the patient *hears* and *sees* is communicated without any modification from the writer, and also without any attribution. We have to assume that there is an omitted ". . . she says that . . .", but with the use of the present there is no tense shift, instead the writer describes the patient in the moment of speaking: ". . . laughs when she relates." The last remark in the report, placed in quotation marks, is recorded once more in a sort of pseudo-direct speech, using the third person.

The note appears to be a careful, measured report of what the patient has described; the narrative follows the patient and her situation closely, and the writer makes no attempt to rush through her version of events to supplant it with his own description of her. Often a characteristic like "vain" is used to conclude such a short note, for the writer to regain control of the patient in the record. Here, however, she is given the last word – albeit in pseudo-direct speech.

The following Status Praesens report also carries long passages of reported speech, but without the use of pseudo-direct speech. The patient is a 37-year-old unmarried female, a pauper. The primary cause of her illness is recorded as "inherited", but "love" is also noted as a cause – albeit in parentheses. It seems that it was not only in the novels of the time that an unhappy affair might lead to suicide, but in the asylums too. The Status Praesens note does not, however, elaborate on these cause of the patient's illness, but includes long passages detailing the background for her admission:

> 14 (1893) [. . .] stat præ.: Her moods are extremely changeable, one minute whimpering and crying and complaining that it will be over for her soon, that it is so dreadful, that it is impossible to hold out; but then her mood can flip extremely quickly, and then she starts smiling rather daftly and is quite cheery. She is very willing to talk about herself, but cannot make sense of her admission here. On the other hand she explains at length about her situation at home; she thought her father and stepmother displayed such peculiar behaviour, that she realised they were trying to poison her. Whenever she went out they used to talk together so suspiciously, she therefore hardly ever dared go out. Besides, her stepmother put poison in her food, and then she used tobacco as an antidote, but then there was poison in the tobacco too, and then she had to use juice and flowers as an antidote. She has no idea about how long ago this started. In particular, there was a dreadful smell in the poorhouse, which was dangerous to her health. She also saw a number of strange things there at night, and that is how someone came to her with the Holy Communion, but whether or not it really was the Communion

she cannot tell, but it struck her as suspicious. Here at the asylum she has neither seen nor heard anything, but on the other hand, she thought one night, that her bedclothes were poisoned. She thinks there are many strange things happening, which she cannot quite fathom, it must be all the others who are mad, because there is nothing wrong with her mind; however she was a little confused at home and she cannot quite understand how it came about that her father ran after her once with a knife. Expression dull, facial features limp.

With the subject so "willing to talk about herself", the writer is given an excellent foundation on which to base such a coherent patient history. There is no doubt, however, that it is rare for patient histories in our material to be presented in such detail. The patient's narrative is preceded by an evaluation of her *mood*; her whimpering and crying alternates with daft smiles and cheeriness. However the narrator does not attempt to elucidate on her alternating moods. Besides this we note the writer's nuanced introductory comments. The three sub-clauses that start with *that*, function as indirect speech attached to the same verb; and all relate to her various complaints. These complaints are linked to the present participles "whimpering" and "crying", which again make up only a part of what we are told are her extremely changeable moods.

A number of *internal causal markers* underpin the logic of the patient's narrative, and contribute to its being coherent and almost uninterrupted within her "vision du monde":

she *thought* her father and stepmother displayed such peculiar behaviour, *that she realised* they were trying to poison her. Whenever she went out they used to talk together so suspiciously, *therefore* she hardly ever dared go out. *Besides*, her stepmother put poison in her food, and then she used tobacco as an antidote, *but then* there was poison in the tobacco too, and then she had to use juice and flowers as an antidote. (italics added)

Here her narrative comes to a halt. We are obliged to understand her statement, "She has no idea about how long ago this started," as an *answer to an unrecorded question*. And again, "Here at the asylum she has neither seen nor heard anything," and "but whether or not it really was the Communion she cannot tell," are also likely to be answers to unrecorded questions. In the extension of the last utterance we get a "but on the other hand", which becomes her subjective extension of the unrecorded question, and she continues, "she thought" as a subjective evaluation not modified by the writer. This brings the patient into a new narrative element, ". . . one night, that her bedclothes were poisoned". Further strengthening the inner coherence of the patient's narrative other elements are introduced, for example "In particular, there was a dreadful smell in the poorhouse", which is instantly related to the patient's own experience and worldview: "which was dangerous to her health".

The section concludes after "knife" with no formal markers of the transition from the patient's text to the writer's: "Expression dull, facial features limp." These formulations are, it seems, such a standard formula, that there is no need for a subject in the sentence. Yet again the subject is omitted. Thus, it is not only the first person "I" that the writer finds difficult to record – in many evaluations and descriptions, once the patient's "voice" falls silent, we lose the subject even in the form of *he* or *she*.

In this example we are confronted for the first time with the problem of a *double voice*. We have already touched on this briefly in connection with the use of free indirect style, in which it is impossible to distinguish the voice of the narrator from that of his subject. But here we see, through the introduction of unrecorded questions, clear indications that the narrative is guided by "the other". On a higher level we have already established the law as an invisible "other", to which the text bows; the patient notes respond to its requirements, even where they remain unspoken. One of the fascinating things about this text is that the questions posed by the other are *not* given such a high prominence in the continuation, because the patient's subjective story lines are not interrupted (It is unlikely this patient note could have been better written today.)

CURIOSA

As mentioned, I have found very few texts throughout this entire 100-year period that attempt to enter the universe of the insane. This omission may be due to the perception of Dementia Praecox as a life only in decline and with little hope of cure. The diagnosis thus forces the writer into passive observation, where the only thing of interest about the patient is his behaviour.

Who are the patients, then, that manage to have their delusions recorded, and who are those who have to content themselves with the dismissive characterisation "no sense to be got from him"? In the entry below, the writer offers us an answer to this question in the shape of a meta-commentary:

> 15a (1893) Is often absorbed in his own musings, speaks rarely with fellow patients, plays chess with himself or wanders about the garden talking in monologues, which occasionally (especially on Sunday mornings) become so loud, that he has to be taken in. His speech is a series of confused opinions, *which are somehow organised into a system and often given the form of a mathematical proof.* [italics added]

It seems that the writer in this instance sees a *recognisable logical form* in the patient's confused opinions. This record continues with a story in which the writer, in the same way as in the Status Praesens above, promotes his own voice as little as possible. He allows the entire entry, after an introductory remark, to fall into a form of pseudo-indirect speech:

> 15b He now relates his life story as follows: "He is not G.G. [his own name]. G.G. was a polytechnic student in Aachen in Westphalia, where he graduated with præceteris non contemnendus. On his journey home he was captured on the 12th degree of latitude; the ship was then brought from the land of the dead to Kristiania [now Oslo] where he had never been. There he, a freeborn innocent, highborn nobleman, was put into a family that resembled [that of] his parents, from there he came to Gaustad possessed with [illegible word], which was at odds with the incorruptibility of the body, as it is God's duty to make sure is maintained in practice. 12 July 1886 at 8 o'clock in the evening [illegible word] he was assassinated by General Skobeleff; his brain was taken out of his head and placed in a blue-painted chest, after which he died and came to the land of the Best. But then the Anti Christ came, here called M. and made something from the food, especially meatballs, to which he added a dialect and a speech device; this work of the Anti Christ was given entry to the nobility and called G.G., which is a mathematically divine possibility, but he is to be called Baron von Meatball. The real G.G. on the other hand, has been resurrected, lives in Stockholm, is 4 years old and unvaccinated and will have a new body and new membrum virile in 10 years time, since the old one is not working."

We read nothing more of this story. It remains as a kind of curiosa, unless perhaps we see the continuation – three years later – as an effort at entering into a dialogue with the patient's delusions:

16 (1896) He laughs loudly when asked, if Baron von Meatball is still alive. "Oh, yes, he is probably still alive. He was a combatant from Juno. There was a battle on Juno, where I was a combatant piece in the game, which was lost by Baron Rosen in a fight against the Anti Christ. G.G. lost 90 000 barrels of innocent blood. God took me back with meat bullion soup and said I was given back with non præceteris or non haud. God takes slices from himself and makes living beings, from which he makes meatballs." Nowadays he does not speak about Baron von Meatball except when he is asked, and he also admits that he has forgotten a lot about all that, since he is often so stupid in his head from all the gunshot wounds. When it is suggested to him that he might ask God, who lives in his head, he says that "God often jumps out of my head, and then I don't have anyone but myself to hold on to."

In this fragment – the maddest in all our material – there is an unusual correspondence between the use of pronouns and direct speech in accordance with grammatical rules.[29] It is fascinating to find the story taken up again after three years of silence. Is the writer simply picking out the best stories? One gets the impression that this man has been a sort of favourite patient at Gaustad, precisely because of his bizarre story, which is both raving mad and also entirely comprehensible. We are reminded once again of Montgomery Hunter's words on the prominence of the anecdote in the hospital environment (*see* above p. 28). Perhaps Baron von Meatball's story is told primarily for the hospital staff so it won't be forgotten, rather than in any attempt to achieve further medical insight into the patient's condition. At one point, the same record enters completely into the imaginings of the patient, in a short note, which is unique to the entire material:

17 (1897) Last night Alexander Dumas's whore came into his bed and danced the can-can; a thing that could not be tolerated either by him or his wife, who is a respectable girl, they then reported this to the head warden, who killed her.

This note is held totally within its own narrative parameters, with no connection to the inter-subjective reality of life in the asylum, apart from its references to "night" and "bed". We hear nothing, for example, of the head

---

29 The alternating between third person to first person in the extract can be assumed to correspond directly to the pattern of the dialogue. Thus the sentence "when asked about [. . .] he answers . . ." would continue in indirect speech, followed by direct speech.

warden, who perhaps calmed the patient in the night; neither are there any modifying expressions that might reveal the distance of the writer to the narrative, or what his points of contact are with the discourse. Any context in which the patient's voice is produced has been removed, something the writer is generally particular about communicating. This story is surely on the borderline of what Gaustad's director, Mr Sandberg, permitted; he always made it clear that the wardens should never refer to the delusions of the mad – and certainly never for humorous effect. Ridicule of the patient's ravings would lead to immediate dismissal. In this entry the patient's *voice* may appear to be rendered very faithfully, but interestingly, because of the absence of any connection between the related story and the person who produced it, the entry appears less patient-focused than the previous one. The story becomes a free-floating anecdote.

THE USUAL DIFFICULT PATIENT

Following these two unusual entries, we will now return to a text that is rather more representative:

> 18 (1891) 43 years, pauper, Stat. Præ.: [. . .] She has kept reasonably calm over the last few days, but is in a state of disorder, she looks confused, keeps her hair untied and is dressed messily; states her year of birth as 1848, but cannot say how old she is, cannot calculate it, "at least not now." She cannot explain how she feels. Her mood has been quite upbeat, she is contented; yet was a little downhearted yesterday. Nothing has been noticed, in either words or deeds, that indicates any suicidal thoughts, and she says herself, apparently sincerely, that she has not had such thoughts "whilst being ill this time".

The evaluative "difficult" and "in a state of disorder" is further substantiated by the three subsequent syntagms: ("confused, "hair untied" and "dressed messily"). In this Status Praesens note too, space is given to speech in quotation marks; its only function, however, is as *confirmation* of the narrator's statement. Since the note starts with the conclusion "difficult and in a state of disorder" it is to be expected that the writing that follows will not pull in the opposite direction. Even the information given by the patient as to her date of birth (which is quite correct) is somehow cast in doubt when the writer tells us that she "states her year of birth as" rather than simply "giving" it as might be expected. Thus her state of physical disorder is transferred onto the linguistic field, but without the note communicating the rationale behind this.

Notions of the patient being "difficult" or "in a state of disorder" as well as "no sense to be had from him/her" are recurring standard formulations of the genre of the psychiatric report during the earliest period of our investigation.

> 19 (1899) 48 years, unmarried, no occupation [. . .] additionally there is no sense to be had from her, maintains that she does not know where she is, *after she has been told.* [italics added]

Here the doctor stresses that there is additionally "no sense to be had from her", suggesting perhaps that the patient is, quite consciously, wriggling out of the structure he has set up for their conversation. This kind of narrative attitude crops up throughout the 100-year period. Even in periods when the writer generally tries to make his discourse inclusive and understanding, the writing sometimes becomes suddenly irritable, and remains so, as soon as there is any suspicion that the patient is not cooperating with the writer in the way he had envisaged.

In this first period the writer rarely reveals his own *set of values* in relationship to what is told, since he virtually *never* leaves traces of his own activities in the text. It is therefore far easier to detect a discrepancy between intention and realisation in the patient notes in recent times, than in the first period.

But even in the records of patients who are "difficult" and from whom "there is little sense to be had", a further image of confusion can be communicated – without comment. The following quote opens, as did the last, by establishing that the patient is "difficult"; but her fragmented speech reflecting this appears at the end of the note, without any comment from the writer. Up to that point the patient's state, of being "difficult", has been hypothesised in an ordered text. Here we observe that the writer does *not*, on the whole, hide his own questioning, on the contrary admits his guiding function in the speech of the other:

> 20 (1899) Stat. Præ.: There is still no sense to be had from her; at times *she does not answer questions, at times she answers no to them all*, withdraws what she has said a moment ago (for instance to the question of whether she is hearing voices, which she confirms initially "without understanding what they are saying".) [. . .]

> *Answers a question* [. . .] she will talk, but is frightened, unable to explain further. "Should not have been here", but does not know where, not in prison, heaven or hell – "in a different village" – "should have taken better care of the others." [italics added]

The patient's three alternative options to hospital; prison, heaven or hell, may either represent answers to questions posed by the writer, or may alternatively have been suggested by the patient without prompting since there is no indication of any hesitation between them. In the first case scenario the questioner must have put in considerable effort, without leaving any trace of this in the text. Irrespective of whether the text originates from the writer or patient, there is no evidence of irritation or impatience in the writing, at the patient's disorganised thinking, as we see expressed in the last quote. A note like this might be a source of inspiration for today's writers: we can see here how a faithful narration of the patient's story seems dependent on the writer being open about his own rhetorical devices.

THE COLLECTIVE BODY

The absence of named *sources* is one of the most defining features of the genre in this first period. The information provided on admission often seems to be provided by an anonymous collective body:

> 21 (1895) 41 years, daughter of manual worker. As a child often sickly [. . .] ten-twelve years ago she became a Methodist. She has been serious, upright, sober and decent.

The image of the patient as serious, upright, sober and decent was probably supplied by the local pillars of the community; the priest, the teacher, the district doctor, the sheriff, and/or close family if they were deemed reliable. Here, the patient's identity is far more rigidly portrayed, and with less opportunity for change than in records closer to our time. Patients *are* this way or that. The image drawn might be complex (cf. the nuanced depiction of the whimpering woman above.) but it is nonetheless unambiguous in that its authority is absolute. Who is behind this information is irrelevant, so long as "he has an unblemished character". A father prone to drink or a mother of ill-repute are, of course, inappropriate sources, since the patient's profile is supposed to be objectively "true". Thus, the collective has a unique opportunity to decide *how a person is* in this first period. Later in our records, the individual will occupy several social spheres and play a variety of roles.

In the following example the collective knowledge of the patient is used to adopt an ironising distance to him:

> 22 (1898) He has occupied himself with reading literature *which is presumed to be above his comprehension*, and with singing exercises *in his more than averagely ordinary singing voice* [. . .] [italics added]

Who is so offended by this "more than averagely ordinary singing voice"? Is this the statement of some condescending connoisseur whose tastes are offended or is it the expression of small-town annoyance at misplaced aspiration, hidden behind a writer's dry irony? Or simply an attempt to foreground the patient's constant overvaluation of his own abilities? Ideally, the third option ought to be the most probable, yet the ironic tone speaks strongly in favour of the first. In these perpetually anonymous character sketches we will, at any rate, never find out. These static character descriptions – whose source is unacknowledged – are very characteristic of the psychiatric notes of the nineteenth century. This can be seen in parallel to the literature of the nineteenth century too. The characters in novels were equipped with certain fixed indicators about which there was no doubt: name, age, family, lineage, profession, geographical belonging, property and fixed characteristics – all designed to give ballast to these fictional characters; the attributes given to people determined who they were. That was, until Knut Hamsun in *Hunger* introduced a character without age, background or sense of belonging, a person without even a name, who simply *exists*, roaming the streets of Norway's capital.

THE INCREASING VISIBILITY OF THE WRITER

By about 1900 it is more common to check the information given in admission notes with the patient. The sort of note we find in one patient file, "the first part of this information is supplied by the patient himself", rarely appears in earlier material. In this same record we find an even stronger indicator of this trend; "detailing her own situation further, she explains . . .". The notes start to indicate more clearly *where* the text is sourced from. The information loses its absolute, objective character. This is paradoxical. In a scientific approach, source referencing is, of course, a sign of non-subjective activity. But by showing under what conditions the writing takes place, the notes appear to be foregrounding the fact that events are not "just as they are". The quote below is a good example, with these objectivity-relativising indicators highlighted:

> 23 (1906) 27 yrs. Pt. arrived from asylum [. . .] *From notes by county physician NN it seems* the pt. *has probably* been shy, and often ill, so that he was held back in his education [. . .] He is dissatisfied with his life, wishes he was dead. He is *presumably* [?] no hallucinations, reports that he sleeps well. Prone to masturbation, has tried to refrain but has begun yet again, *allegedly* to weaken himself. [. . .] [italics added]

The referencing of sources together with the use of modifying adverbial phrases can only mean that the writer's contact with an external reality is less reliable and subject to some doubt, which the writing must mirror. After the turn of the century we find the writer referring to himself, as in the admission note below:

> 24 (1909) 46 yrs. widow of smallholder [. . .] As an adult she has been a hard worker, but has always liked to have fun, dancing and the like. [. . .] *When I looked in on her*, she was resting. [. . .] She had seen so many nasty things, including an old, black man and had heard voices that said they wanted to kill her, was therefore frightened. She talked about a brother in America who had placed something electric on her, whether this was to harm or heal her, *I could not quite tell* [signed by district doctor]. [italics added]

The writer takes a far from dominant place in this text, and does not problematise his presence. The writer's "I" is not placed in the text to facilitate alternative readings. He is a fully *reliable narrator*, and need do no more than draw a discrete attention to himself to be heard. He is present so as to identify the origin of some of the information within the text.

The notion of a "reliable author" comes from a pre-narratological classic, Wayne Booth's *The Rhetoric of Fiction*. Booth distinguishes between the reliable and the unreliable narrator. The unreliable narrator gives a "faulty" account of events in the story, and it is the reader's task to decipher the content of the text in such a way as to not misinterpret it. Ideally the author and reader should interpret the text in the same way, bypassing, so to speak, the unreliable author. Many use the concept "immanent author" or "implied author" for the system of norms which the text expresses. Ideally the implied author should, in our text examples, generally coincide with the manifest narrator, who I call the writer. But this is not the case. We have already seen how the writer believes he is expressing something that the text's cumulative system of norms actually questions. I will not make use of Booth's concepts directly in what follows; it will be clear from the context what I mean by implied author and unreliable narrator, when we have need of the terms. But to separate the narrator's direct expressions from the text's system of norms is a fundamental distinction. The linking of information to its sources may be seen as a display of doubt about the information offered, but it manifests itself quite automatically; the doubt is not based on any deep-felt conviction. Rather, the impression is that the writer is now *expected* to refer to his sources, as above, without being overly concerned about it.

The text fragment below comes from a patient note in which the difficulties in getting information about the patient's family are very obvious. Nonplussed, the writer continues giving other information which we must assume originates from the inhabitants of the patient's village, local gossip so to speak, which shows no trace of any relativising attitude to the truth of what is told.

It has been suggested that a form of "public opinion" constitutes the narrator's voice for large stretches of Charles Dickens' humorous and colourful novels.[30] The "common sense" of society speaks through the narrator in Dickens, as it does through this writer at Gaustad hospital:

> 25 (1914) Mother a vagrant, now pauper and beggar, lives with her son (the pt.) in a wretched little hut. Pt. was born out of wedlock; father was a sailor. Pt. was aggressive as a child and when growing up. Was neither peculiar nor introvert, at times uncontrollable. After his confirmation he went to sea for a while, but has for many years now lived at home with his mother and been mainly occupied with the making of wicker baskets, but has not wanted to participate in any proper work, has trekked around with a hunting rifle and done some fishing [. . .].

---

30 Mikhail Bakhtin uses the term in *Du discours romanesque*. The characters' linguistic zones can be seen as standing in dialogue with "public opinion" in some nineteenth century realism.

Social prejudices govern the progress of this text. The "occupation" of the mother is not limited to vagrant and pauper; she is also a beggar. Their dwelling is described by a non-neutral adjective, "wretched". He doesn't go hunting, but treks around "with a hunting rifle", a description that underscores his good-for-nothing character. In the world of the writer there are unspecified differences between "work" and "proper work". The patient doesn't manage more than to be "occupied with the making of . . .". He has had, according to the writer, a choice, but has not wanted to participate in any proper work". Is it the case that a naturalistic outlook also strengthens an *a priori* understanding of the individual; that a kind of mutually reinforcing effect is going on here; that the more one expresses ones social prejudices, the more one strengthens a view of the lower classes as locked in by inheritance and environment? If so, how are the prejudices of today expressed? Or do the writers of today feel that they have reached a level where this question is no longer apposite?

THE PRINCE AND THE PAUPER

One of the ways that social difference is expressed in the records of the 1890s is that a greater amount of text is given to patients of higher status than to those who are more "ordinary". In the fragment below, the patient asks repeatedly for a meeting with the director, until the hospital tires of her:

26 (1895) Asked yesterday to speak with the director in confidence. Explains that there are many voices speaking in her chest, which troubles her hugely. It is a "good voice" that has instructed her to explain this alone and one-to-one with the director. She feels a lot of pain for this good voice, since other voices hurl dreadful swear words at it, calling it "you lowlife scoundrel", which is just so very dreadful, she says. [. . .] Last evening she asked yet again to speak with the director, reported that she was charged with telling [them] that her good voice belonged to the best man in the land, namely Dr. M. and added that she felt much more calm [. . .]

1½ years later: [. . .] has "seen a dream vision, wherein a blue knight was revealed to her in the shape of the assistant doctor, wherefore he must become her saviour"; she always pleads to be allowed to explain herself in confidence. But when [this request] is granted, *she cannot work out what she was supposed to say; the whole thing disintegrates into foolish prattle.* [italics added]

The patient has been given the privilege of having a one-to-one dialogue with the director. Her two voices are described in very ordered language. But the conscientious writer does not enter into this note as in some of the previous ones; her *linguistic zone* is prevented from spreading in the first section by a "she says" within a passage, already cautiously marked as indirect speech. Further down, quotation marks are placed around third person remarks. By the end of the last note patience has run out. Being allowed a meeting in confidence requires certain standards. The patient does not manage this. The patient is virtually required to communicate her madness with no nonsense if she wishes to bother the upper ranks of the hospital staff. Where other notes end in there being "no sense to be had" from the patient, this one ends in "foolish prattle."

The collective and anonymous voice that the writer sometimes employs, always relies on the prevailing "common sense" of the day. The quote below comes from the admission notes of a convict. He is to be assessed for insanity. At this point in history we find "prisoner" listed under "occupation". This is not, it seems, a temporary state; it cannot be expected "to pass" or change. People are who they are, and one's characteristics are fixed for all time. Consequently the temperament of the convict is evident in all his activities. In the following extract the writer seems convinced of the patient's evil; so very different from how a young man would be assessed today:

27 (1891) Occupation: Convict. Transported from XX penal institution [. . .] From his notes from ZZ mental asylum the following is entered: Father has been a very heavy drinker. Mother very nervous; a half sister on his mother's side and a brother are insane. As a small child he was awkward and short-tempered; became worse as he grew up in spite of warnings and punishments; the smallest instance could provoke a terrible temper, [he] was obstinate, indecent in words and behaviour; was cruel to other children and took pleasure in seeing them cry; was arrogant and [illegible]; impetuous and ill-tempered; heartless to those closest to him. At school he was disobedient; but showed reasonable abilities. Has since been in many types of business and apprenticeships, but because of [his] unpredictability, unreliability, obstinacy and violent nature he has always been fired. Has always sought poor company, has masturbated, been drawn to drink and hung out with prostitutes.

Who is the source of all this information? The high status patient in the previous example was described in far more individual terms, perhaps also because her *daughter* came through in the record very much as an individual and as having given nuanced information. Here in this report, however, we meet a person who is *evil through and through*. He has been obstinate, indecent, cruel, arrogant, impetuous, ill-tempered, heartless and violent, no less. There is not the least doubt attached to *any one* of these numerous characteristics. He has also *always* sought *poor company*, masturbated, been drinking and hung out with prostitutes. The writer's pleasure lies in formulating this endless list of negative characteristics. In the 1890s, insanity, "delicate nerves" and alcoholism in the family, all serve to guarantee that the writer is on the right track in his portrait, caught as he is in a naturalistic worldview. Consequently he lets loose a stream of unsubtle characteristics, and reserves his more nuanced approach for the more deserving cases.

The convict in this fragment is additionally suspected of *simulating* insanity elsewhere in his file. In other words, the writer is worried about being taken for a ride, something that hardly exerts much pressure to change the tone in a more moderate direction.

The introductions of these records are formulaic. Some patients have always been *difficult*. Some have been *well behaved* once, and have then become *difficult* since. If in the introduction lasciviousness, drink, poverty or insanity are implied to run in the family, we can be sure that much ill has befallen the offspring, that is, the patient, and a certain condescending attitude towards these people on the part of the writer tends to follow in the remainder of the notes. It is obvious – even if Sandberg's guidelines do not put huge emphasis on inheritance as a factor in mental illness – that when a report's introduction points to negative circumstances in the family, traces of this will be found in the subsequent notes about the patient.

Around 1915 it has become common to give the names and occupations of parents. Previously, one only wrote "farmer's daughter", "blacksmith's wife" etc. when the patient him or herself had no occupation. Recording the names of parents can be seen as a way of bringing the family closer to the patient. As mentioned above, Dr Sandberg regarded it as liberating for the patient to escape the domestic environment. This tendency of naming parents trails off again some years later. Famous family members, however, are always noted: "Prof. Dr. B. informs us that the [patient's] mother was the daughter of the ex Member of Parliament, NN, and that her siblings are drinkers."

In the extract below, the patient (a postal worker) is consistently referred to by his first name, despite being 33 years of age. This must be judged against his poor family background. A respectable job is not enough to give sufficient social status. The difference in status between the writer and patient is, incidentally, *never* a topic in the 100-year period covered by this research. Using first names for adult persons becomes usual in the 1970s, although one can see a certain disinclination to this in present times.

> 28) Mother of nervous disposition and suffers from melancholy, an older sister has suffered from religious aspirations for about a year, brother was "nuvvus" bordering on the insane, for a period of about 4 months after being afflicted with pneumonia. Father fairly prone to drink [. . .] He [the patient] has always been a fearful type (afraid of the dark). Has masturbated, otherwise nothing noteworthy during formative years. As an adult fairly prone to drink. About a year ago had a love affair that went awry.

Even before any record is made of the patient's condition, inheritance, drink and masturbation are cited as causes of his illness, whilst information is also supplied to the effect that his mother has a nervous disposition and suffers from melancholy. Additionally the brother is "nuvvus" and the father prone to drink. Interestingly, the writer has chosen to highlight the patient's own accent; his brother is described as "nuvvus" after being "afflicted" with pneumonia. Here the writer mixes institutional, scientific hospital jargon, the norm, with the outsider's non-adapted language, which is necessarily put in inverted commas. The mix is made up of such heterogeneous elements, that there is no risk of the patient's voice spreading further into the text and getting the upper hand, as we have observed elsewhere.

Women *suffer* from *unhappy love*, while the man in this example has had a *love affair that went awry*. There is, then, less emotional depth in this patient. This leads us to speculate whether it is gender or social class that is the determining factor in the way instances of love are related. In other patient files we see male lecturers and rentiers suffering from unhappy love. In the same way, frivolous servant girls might occasionally have love affairs that go awry. It would have been interesting to know who produced the image of the patient as "an adult fairly prone to drink".

The descriptive categories that are employed in this first period are, as we have seen, limited in nuance; very often they revolve around "good" versus "bad", "difficult" versus "well-behaved", as in the following example:

> 29 (1901) 22 years. 4 years ago she started to become so obstinate and *difficult* at home, that she had to be put with strangers; but nothing came of it. She was admitted last year to a hospital where she improved, participated in work and was *well behaved*. This spring she went home for a while, but became so *unreasonable, obstinate and difficult* again, that she was readmitted to hospital [. . .] [italics added]

The categorisations are partly socially determined. People from higher echelons of society are rarely either good or bad. That is not to say that "simple terms" cannot also give an adequate description. In this note socially determined elements are considerably more pronounced in the Status Praesens description. It is interesting that when the description does not focus on insanity, the moral distance between patient and writer becomes increasingly clear. In the example below we even see a hint of erotic fascination on the part of the writer:

> 30) Stat. Praes.: Fully mature with a blossoming appearance. Vain and giddy, cries and laughs interchangeably, does not fix her thoughts on anything.

To what extent is it specific to her that she does not "fix her thoughts on anything"? Might there really not be *anything* behind her vanity and giddiness that could resemble a thought process worthy of investigation? The rejection of her as a "thinking" person stands in stark contrast to the lustful desire the writer exhibits in his description of her as "fully mature with a blossoming appearance". It is as if the writer's physical attraction is kept in check by the rejection of the patient as a person.

CAUSE AND EFFECT

In one record that opens with a cause of illness related to "masturbation", the condition is referred to again further down in a short entry of two sentences:

> 31 (1903) Has stopped masturbating. Not hearing as many voices as before.

The *coupling* of these two sentences is fascinating. There is a cause and effect relationship between them which is left unpronounced, but which is nonetheless persuasive. For the readers of the day these two things were doubtless closely linked, in line with the unspoken intentions of the writer.

The message is that a causal factor of the disease is no longer present. If the cause is removed, we can expect improvements!

The link between two such statements – hidden as it is – can be difficult to detect in notes whose content is less clear cut. But in this case it seems quite blatant: To patient and writer of 1903, masturbation is a codeword for obsessive behaviour, which, as soon as it is mentioned, flags an important turn in the text.

Today's writer would have had to make quite a few intricate internal links to make us accept any correlation between "no more masturbation" and "no more hallucinations". This use of unstated, but nonetheless persuasive, links will be used later in the twentieth century, when the effects of electroshock and lobotomy are described, when the procedure is described in one sentence, and in the next sentence certain afflictions have grown less pronounced. Indeed, as a genre, the psychiatric record is characterised by such unpronounced text, suggesting causal connections that can be interpreted in the "best" direction, but which – on closer inspection – turn out to be placed in the text in such a way that the writer cannot be blamed for having promised anything. When two statements are as disassociated from each other as these are to the modern reader, the narrative technique becomes exposed. Yet it is reasonable to assume that today's writers are equally prone to such techniques, even if these are more difficult for us to identify, inhabiting, as we do, the same world. But perhaps the writer has an awareness himself when he is in the process of creating such a text, as unscientific as it might seem reasonable on the surface.

THE TEXT THAT STEERS ITSELF

Should an introduction be too much at variance with the norm, we know immediately that the variant textual element has a specific significance. For example, in the following record, in the space for "insanity and criminal history in the family" it says that the father and brother are jealous:

> 32 (1896) Parents smallholders. His father and brother have been known in the village for being very jealous.

Just a few lines on and the reader gets the pleasure of having a cause/effect structure confirmed when it states "he [the patient] goes round in the village talking about his wife's "unfaithfulness." Like father like son.

When, in an 1894 file, we read under a heading "suicide or crime in the family" that the patient's father was convicted for "whoredom or concubinary", we are primed to accept that the cause of illness is "grief over the illegitimate child (born prior to marriage) who has turned out badly." The sins of the father.

Circumstances regarded as important during one particular period of a patient's stay can be brought out again at a later date, and used to explain events that have happened in the intervening period. In such cases the doctor's perception of the patient is influenced by the notes that are already written about him. Again, this is more difficult for us to spot in notes from our own day, since the markers in these texts can so easily seem to confirm that "that's how things are". But as modern readers, we have enough distance to aspects of the nineteenth century naturalistic worldview to find it easier to interpret the facts of that period as textual signals aimed at providing coherence in the narrative.

WRITING IN SOLIDARITY

The function of the seemingly random, yet poignant, daily notes about patients' everyday activities is to chart any changes in the patient's condition. When well-written, such fragments can remind us that the patient is a person and they often carry added value. The notes spring out of individual situations and from single individuals, but in their uncommented form they can also say something universal, as in the case of the succinct note below on suffering:

> 33 (1904) Destroyed a table today, *because* she was angry at having to suffer more than other people. [italics added]

As a reader one is fascinated by the internal motivation ("because") which the writer sees no reason to distance himself from.

And a similar inclusive attitude can be glimpsed in the following note:

> 34 (1890) She has been calm and well-behaved for some time now, is fairly productive in her handicraft, but has been easily offended and hot tempered on occasion, especially when she has been reprimanded; was out with the others yesterday, became suddenly agitated for no understandable reason, tore her umbrella and hat to pieces and said words to the effect that she wanted to hang herself.

Might there be a risk in allowing oneself be seduced by texts that are well written? Of perhaps romanticising or sentimentalising the narrative? Is it romanticising in this instance, to look past the madness of the patient, and read the text as if it were about somebody who is not mad? Yet, surely, this happens consistently in our material, all the way to the present day. Surely the "difficult and bad patient who eventually becomes pleasantly and skilfully absorbed in some gainful activity" comprises the basic plot of any successful hospital story, told in different words in different times. The insane are described in the language of the sane. So long as I admit to the pleasure I gain from a good text and do not try to hide it, the tendency to romanticise is kept in check. It is important, as mentioned earlier, that I do not get stuck in a certain perspective, and that in the presentation of the text corpus I allow my changing sympathies and antipathies as a reader to be visible, so as to illuminate the genre in as nuanced a way as possible.

The fragment above is one of my favourites. It dates from 1890, yet the woman who "for no understandable reason" tears her hat and umbrella to pieces and proclaims her desire to hang herself, could have been a character in a 1970s Beckett play. The writer admits that this violent reaction takes place for no *understandable* reason, that is, there is *probably* some explanation or other for her behaviour; certainly the writer does not exclude this possibility, but his attitude in what he tells us is that, to him at least, it is inexplicable He describes these events respectfully in relation to the unexplained inner state of the patient (without commenting on the loss of an expensive umbrella). The writer accepts her existential rage, despite not understanding it. The real reason for this rage we do not know. The woman – calmly walking with the others – has had *enough* – and rids herself of the symbols of a well-ordered existence that she has about her person. The protest is silent and furious. Her exclamations about wanting to hang herself are only sketched in, the writer sums them up in one single clause, but the core content that she wants to hang herself, is indisputable.

One of things that makes me "fall" for this extract as a reader, is its matter-of-fact style, despite its moving towards an existential extreme. The fragment is neatly divided into two symmetric halves, divided by the main punctuation mark (the semicolon). The first part is clearly iterative, the second just as clearly singulative; first we are presented with the fact that she has behaved normally "for some time", then we are told about this single, exceptional instance. We have already seen, in other patient notes, that the iterative passages are often set in the present tense, as if to underline the perpetual (e.g. piano-playing in the air). Here, however, the iterative is kept in the past. Thus the writer gives the single event even more importance. Having once torn the items to pieces, it is in no way certain that she will return to her "fairly productive handicraft". The singulative section becomes an expression of something inevitable that pulls the rug from beneath the previously idyllic, iterative calm. It is the destruction of the hat and the umbrella which we *see*, and towards which the entry as a whole points.

The teller tells, from a safe distance to that which is told. "She has been calm and well-behaved for some time now." The "time" referred to here will, from now on, belong firmly in the past. A disquieting unease is sketched out after the first comma: She has been no more than *fairly* productive in her handicraft, and she has not shown herself to be just easily offended, but *rather* easily offended.

Despite the distance to the patient's world being clearly marked, the teller nonetheless relies on the reader's capacity to identify with the patient. Who amongst us is more than "fairly" productive? And which of us might not get *rather* easily offended and hot-tempered if we felt humiliated by being reprimanded?

The singulative story, in its concluding three lines, contains everything needed for the description to be understood at other times and other places; the context, the walk with "the others" (in the world of the mad), in contrast to her artefacts – the hat and the umbrella – tokens of a connection to the ordered world; the statements about hanging herself, which come as an answer to the Camusesque existentialist problem – suicide or not, and finally the tearing apart, the furious revolt – inexplicable to all, including the writer.

Samuel Beckett would have ended his text here. But the record writer goes on:

> 35) Later she was giddy, almost silly, in quite a lively mood and declaring that she meant nothing at all of what she had said. She has apparently said that she was going to strangle herself before.

Only in flashes is existence as clear as in the moment of action when the outburst took place "for no apparent reason". Six months later, her story can be concluded.

36) Has remained stable and well behaved for a long time; participated diligently and with interest in a number of house activities. Patient discharged cured.

With such accolades, she is surely deserving of the most positive of discharge notes.

4

Second period: 1920–50

THE MATERIAL

From around 1910 more writing space is given over to the doctor's investigations. The doctor now engages more actively with the information that is recorded on the patient's admission. A fuller body of textual material results; the single pages assigned to each patient in the leather-bound casebooks each year are not always sufficient. The reader is forced to leaf forwards and backwards in the annals to find the continuation of a record. The format bursts from within, and loose, individual patient files are introduced.

The diverse voices that speak through the writer have both a *synchronic* and *diachronic* dimension. If the patient has a long history of illness, the report will contain notes from different periods. Now that the notes are kept in individual files these become one continuous story. The writer now becomes better acquainted with the way other writers have written before him, which is a clue to understanding the conservative inclinations of the writing.

Additionally, during the 1930s we find that files are catalogued according to the date of discharge rather than the date of admission. This has resulted in the overrepresentation of some years in my research; it has not always been possible to limit the analysis to notes from one and the same period. I preferred, during my reading at Gaustad Hospital, to follow a report to its conclusion. This may mean that the macro-level divisions are less obvious, but the analysis is less fragmented when following a patient-story from beginning to end. Whatever the case, the division into the three main periods before our present time, is meant as an aid in organising a large corpus, and locating tendencies and through-lines in historical material. These divisions are not, of course, absolute.

THE ART OF THE SHORT NOTE

The short notes about the patients and the everyday goings on at the asylum are less prevalent in the new files. Yet, when they are well written, unique pictures of people and situations emerge, like palimpsests. The short note is no longer merely concerned with recording changes in the patient's condition. Sometimes the ward round comes to a halt, and the light of attention is allowed to fall on an otherwise almost forgotten patient – or the writer may indulge in a detailed description of a situation. The following impressionistic sketch was drawn as late as in 1950:

> 1 (1950) During the rounds today the pt. greets the doctor and explains that she calls herself Jenny John. "Am I not called Tanja Tøyen?" "I walk very quietly through life hiding everything." (Is that tiring?) "It's no fun at the clinic, but I don't think about it," she says. She is untidy but not unhygienic now. She spends time in the knitting room in the afternoons. (Any strange experiences?) "No, I don't see anything." She says she's happy here. She behaves politely, does not speak impulsively, but it is incoherent and incomprehensible.

The kindly question "Is that tiring?" does not carry any hope of an answer that might imply any change in her condition. But by asking the question the writer has found a linguistic field within which he and the patient can communicate, each out of their respective expectations. Many of the records that cover long-term patients from around 1950 have a sense of stagnation about them. Neither patient nor writer seem to have any particular expectations. This is, however, different in the records where electroshock therapy or lobotomy hover in the background as a unexpressed possibility. In such cases it seems that the writer is no longer interested in "innocuous" inconsequential notes. This is not so strange perhaps; the scientific value of the above note is negligible – so long as one has no interest in the actual content of a patient's delusions. But what is psychiatrically of interest is, after all, only one aspect of the patient's life at the asylum.

The writer as text maker can sometimes give the impression of being entirely familiar with contemporary fiction writers. This is also true in the oldest records, where we see narrative devices that fiction writers have been famed for (e.g. iterative quotes, *see* p. 50). Beneath the surface of the next fascinating note we see hints of the "new documentary style", the Scandinavian proponents of which were Arthur Omre and Gunnar Larsen in the 1930s:

2 (1946) Hid himself behind a cupboard door and snatched the keys from a nurse looking for some papers for another patient. Quick as a flash he unlocked both main doors, let himself out and disappeared with the bundle of keys. Nurse managed swiftly to sound the alarm and one of the staff came running, gave chase, but did not succeed in catching the patient. Matron spoke to T. just beforehand, and then he said that he had no need to be here anymore and his place would be better taken by somebody else. He seemed agitated. At 8 a.m. a report came from the sheriff of S. concerning a man that matched the description of T, who was brought into custody around 1.30 last night. 3 wardens have been sent to collect him.

Just as the story of the escape has been established, there follows a retrospective account of the situation earlier that evening, thus creating a pause in the dramatic events. This therefore becomes the natural moment to communicate something about the mood of the patient, as it was just before the story's action, *in medias res* (or: in mid-affairs). *In medias res* is a very common structural device in prose fiction: the narrative begins in the middle of a suspenseful situation, the explanation for which is given retrospectively at a calmer point in the story. This device was developed in the realistic novel of the nineteenth century. Interestingly, we did not come across this form in the first period, where we find a more "saga-like" depiction of events, if – and I stress *if* – the patient is recognised as an individual at all. The norm of the notes in the first period was as follows: first background explanations, followed by iterative situation, before the singulative event. The short notes of the nineteenth century tended instead to focus on the patient as part of the asylum, for example, in the example of the depersonalised screeching.

Escapes are always described with an eye to the possible legal ramifications, but the richness of detail in the opening sentences of this quote must be put down to the writer's joy in storytelling. The nurse who forgets to look after her keys as she searches for letter paper in the cupboard, is one of the countless images that have brought the asylum alive for me, throughout this 100-year period. This is, of course, not the aim of the report genre, yet this note succeeds at it all the same; this does not make it misleading or unworthy of being imitated by other report writers in later periods. It is in particular the writer's focus on the situation there and then, with a willingness to include contextual details and simultaneously not lose the through-line of the story, which remains impressive half a century later.

In the 1940s, records have an entry field for a "Yearly Summary". The term says a great deal about the form of writing one might expect. Against such a stagnant background, the above *in medias res* story strikes one as even more action-packed. The following note, written almost 20 years after a patient's admission, comes from a record which, on the whole, contains nothing more than short yearly summaries that have little more to report than the lack of any change in the patient's condition:

> 3 (1962) Her condition stays the same from year to year. She is kindly, calm and of a friendly disposition and in her way a charming woman.

There is a kind of warmth in the concluding words of this note. Such formulations become less frequent in later periods, since increasingly the patient's potential charm is only assessed in relation to norms *outside* the hospital. This woman has her own value *inside* the collective of the hospital; mad as she is, she is *charming in her way*. In the previous period we saw texts in which the screeches of a patient were detached from the individual person, but were a part of the asylum's overall din. People were, both then and in this quote, valued within the context of the system itself. Troubling on the one hand perhaps, yet simultaneously beautiful when the warmth of a moment shines through the writer's discourse.

In this period the writer shows a growing ability and willingness to formulate precise, detailed descriptions of situations and patients; including those that do not have anything verbal to communicate:

> 4 (1933) Pt. quiet and peaceable, causes no trouble [. . .]

Perhaps this is the exact goal? That the patient should not cause trouble. The use of the present tense underscores the absence of dynamism. The note continues:

> 5) [. . .] keeps herself to herself, has sat in her place in the workshops for approx 1 year, sewing strips of cloth together, automatically and disinterestedly.

The note is reminiscent of others from the 1890s. "sat in her place [. . .] for approx 1 year" illustrates the infernally static and unchanging situation to which those with chronic psychiatric illnesses are subjected. Additionally, the meaninglessness of the task of sewing strips of cloth together is highlighted for both reader and writer. An uncritical writer would probably have called it "making bedspreads". Seen from the patient's point of view it is probably quite accurate to describe the work carried out automatically and disinterestedly, yet this statement also contains the writer's identification with the futility of the activity.

The phrase "causes no trouble" vouches for the system and defends its continuance. The hospital may have an interest in the situation remaining static: as we will see, those patients who are least ill are the ones who are most bothersome to the asylum; their differentness represents a disturbance. Paradoxically, we come closer here to the idea that the asylum has a preference for the chronically ill, at least during those periods when it is able to offer a fixed number of beds for indefinite periods.

Information sources are identified with greater regularity in the short notes during this period; although the individual names of sources are not given, we are at least supplied with their job titles:

> 6 (1927) Was very troubled last night, kicked at the door, given med. at 12 a.m. She liked the medicine very much, *said the nurse*, she thought she might "fall asleep forever"; – and she wouldn't have minded that at all. [italics added]

Previously in a statement such as "she liked the medicine very much" there would have been no subject (she) and nothing to indicate who had supplied the information. In the early years at Gaustad, not even sources from *the outside world* were attributed. Events, both inside and outside the institution were as they were. In being attributed, in this case to a nurse, the information loses its value as a wholly objective fact. We observe a certain kind of *dissolving* of the image of the unified hospital. The notes lose their secure authoritative aura. Previously things *were* exactly as they appeared in the text. Now we have a mere nurse reporting. Nevertheless, this short note allows the patient's "vision du monde" to dominate the text – rather frighteningly maybe. And yet the hospital is still so confident of its own authority and of having the situation under control, that the writer does not need to have the last word in order to add, as Ekdal in *The Wild Duck*, that such a thing (the patient's final sleep) would never be allowed to happen. Not until our own time will we find such interventions.

THE LAB-INVESTIGATIONS OF THE 1920s

During the 1920s we come across what is perhaps the most unique, single feature of the genre throughout the 100-year period: the so-called *Lab-investigation*; for which entire conversations between the doctor and patient were recorded. Here we find ample use of direct speech; far more than either before or since. The occasional very lengthy medical examinations, recorded after 1910, may well have been some kind of precursor to the Lab-investigations, but whereas these were predominantly somatically motivated, the Lab-investigations centred on the talking itself and must have been recorded stenographically. This format disappears again in the 1930s.[31]

The Lab-investigation is so unique that it is worth giving a substantial example:

> 7 (1924) Lab. Polite, readily volunteers information. (so why have you come here, then?) "Well, the nurse said I should come here." (why did you come to Gaustad?) "– don't know – for the hypnosis." (what do you mean, the hypnosis?) "a kind of sleep – half way – like a semi-sleep" – "and that comes from [the word] hypnosis, which means sleep." (Have *you* had a lot to do with hypnosis?) Well, no, not really." (Have you been exposed to hypnosis?) [. . .] "Then father spoke about taking a Christmas holiday, I thought it was a bit early" (and then?) "then I stayed up at night smoking . . ." in connection to the q. of sexual matters he says: "well, and then there's the religious connection too" (Is there a connection between the religious and the sexual?) "Yes, absolutely" (?) "Well, the Salvation Army – there you have both" (On which night did NN [school friend] influence him?) – he thinks it was the night of the 15th or 16 October. last year, he was awake in the night then – "the erotic was part of it – with the masturbation" (did NN have anything to do with it?) "Yes, I had that feeling." (How?) "Well, he lives quite close, at X." – (?) "It seems to me it was thought or emotion transfer" – "it was him NN, who awakened erotic feelings in me" (Had there been no such feelings before?) He believes that NN

---

31 Skålevåg is also fascinated by this format, both because it has a linguistic focus and because it is so unusual: "In the 'lab-investigation' of the 1920s [. . .] we find traces of a psychiatry which is interpretive, where the objects of interpretation are not primarily somatic signs, but language" (Skålevåg, 2003, p. 122). "It is worth noting that the 'lab-investigations' were, as far as I know at least, never mentioned in any professional journals or other publications. These were part of an investigatory process, a methodology, which nobody ever tried to market. We find here a truth about the mind which has some medical relevance that can only be communicated by words" (ibid, p. 124).

had consumption – X was not a healthy place. – NN had a weakness for women, he behaved so openly and showily, "behaved so strangely towards me". This is in answer to a question on the thought transfer from NN to patient. (Why did NN get the patient to masturbate that night?) "I don't know, that might have been his plan too" – then he says there probably was no plan, and he adds that it "had to be poverty" – (In what way?) "Well, he looked very poorly". (What would NN gain or achieve from that?) – he mentions that NN was created to differentiate between friends (how?) he then speaks of his brothers "He (NN) believed that I was much bigger since I was a student" (bigger than who?) – he smiles here, as he often does, (bigger than who?) "Bigger than E.W. for example." (Who is E.W.?) "that's my brother" He doesn't really think NN wanted him to masturbate, but that he (pt.) grew more self-conscious after having got to know NN, and that night he felt a "pull towards him (NN) "(of love?) "Yes" (was the pull [you felt] to NN of an erotic nature?) "Yes, there is no doubt about that" – it is not easy for him to tell whether it was in a woken state or half-sleep (Have you felt a similar erotic pull to women?) "Yes, sometimes", "not very much – it is both" (are you fond of dancing?) "No, I can't dance."

Here, the patient's attitude is described *before* his voice is introduced; a pattern we recognise from the previous period. The fact that the text opens with the patient being both polite *and* willing to speak, reassures the reader that the text will not deteriorate in the direction of his being "difficult" or that "no sense is to be had from him" or, indeed, that the doctor will be called a bastard!

The interlocutor's questions are put in parentheses; a graphic indication that the patient is meant to stand out in the text. The doctor/writer hides from view, and this is done in such a way that we do *not* expect sudden "surprise assaults" against the patient. Yet we observed previously in the Hamsun record, that despite his parenthetical position, Dr Langfeldt succeeded in revealing layers in the patient which, for good reason, he tried to keep back. The use of parentheses around questions is a consistent feature of the genre, and continues to this day. Generally there are no more than one or two questions, and they soon give the writer the opportunity to come out of the parenthesis and regain control of the discourse.

An important theoretical issue associated with such recorded dialogue, is the question of how much of the speech is directed towards the interlocutor and how much towards the potential reader outside the conversation. This is a familiar problem, not least in drama theory and analysis. Perhaps it was this complication that ultimately caused the Lab-investigations to be regarded as too subjective, since the form is too artificial for satisfactory two-way communication. Nevertheless these conversations stand out for their intimacy and respect, and for the interest they reveal in the individuality of the patient. In the last chapter we saw examples of patients' speech being steered by unrecorded questions. Viewed purely linguistically, the inclusion of the laboratory questions in parentheses seems a more accurate form of reporting.

For once, it is not essential for the writer to have control of the direction of the conversation. We can already see in the first question – [. . . (so why have you come here, then?) "Well, the nurse said I should come here." (why did you come to Gaustad?) "- don't know – for the hypnosis."] The narrator *could* have summed up here and said that the patient had misunderstood the first question so as to move the interview on more quickly. But it does not seem that the writer has a particular goal towards which he wants to guide the conversation. The dialogue is a goal *in itself*.

When the patient in the quote above stops or hesitates mid-sentence, this is also recorded, not through meta-commentary, but with the inclusion of the doctor's interjections ["Then father spoke about taking a Christmas holiday, I thought it was a bit early" (and then?) "then I stayed up at night smoking . . ."]

That said, the text has been subject to editing. Long sections of dialogue are, for example, given in indirect speech: [. . . "I don't know, that might have been his plan too" – *then the patient says that there was probably no plan, and adds that it* "had to be poverty"] Additionally there are some comments of an iterative nature: [he smiles here, *as he often does*]. This comment is in fact a straight forward addition. The questioner repeats the exact same question immediately afterwards. The writer cloaks his question about sexuality and chooses an indirect formulation: [in connection with the q. of sexual matters he says: ". . ."] Historically it is fascinating to see how homosexual love is given an acceptable framework: it is linked to masturbation – which was still seen as a *causal factor* in the illness. The patient's masturbation is also connected with the thought transfer from a person of the same gender to whom he feels an "erotic pull". One valuable dimension of this conversational format is the way it moves gradually towards what is a sensitive issue. The writer backs off however at a certain point, asking the bizarre question; "are you fond of dancing?"

When it comes to the theme of homosexuality, cultural stereotypes and clichés are not, in retrospect, hard to recognise. It is indicated in this patient's record that he liked to play at theatre as a child. This is presented later in the record as a stimulus for the sexual perversion, and bolsters the idea of the homosexual as a theatrical being – without this ever being brought to the text's surface:

> 8) About 1 year ago he was very involved in play acting and art generally and took great interest in it. He started posing in front of the mirror for long periods and practicing mimetic exercises and playing the fool in front of his brothers and sisters. His father rebuked him for this occasionally. (From the admission notes, same patient)

The following description of a violent scene in the patient's home is fairly standard, but the concluding remark breaks with convention, and is significant for this particular patient:

> 9) In the morning he was raging – chased his mother and a brother out of the house [. . .] *Behaviour totally theatrical.* [italics added]

This gives the impression of being *a cohesive text* when in fact a seemingly random factor seems almost to act as a leitmotif. This can lead the reader to associations of a naturalistic worldview again, as when the introductions of older records implied that the madness of parents manifested itself in their offspring. Yet this repetition and sense of inescapable destiny may equally stem from the writer's need to make the text assume a *form*. Is it the text that steers itself, or is it the writer's own worldview that suddenly shines through?

What makes the dialogues in the records of the 1920s so different from the notes of the present day is that they lack any medical and sociological *jargon*. These patients have not yet started to use *medical language* – unlike those of today who we see regularly labelling themselves as, for example, psychotic.

But the Lab-investigations require a certain *intellectual concordance* between doctor and patient to work at their best. The last patient was a student; the patient below is a shop assistant. This time the doctor's opening question is; "What is the problem?"; clearly a less inviting approach than the open-ended "so why have you come here, then?" seen above. The dialogue continues:

10) (Had you been drunk beforehand?) "Not much – excuse me, who am I speaking to?" (polite) Married 10 years, childless. Last year he spent 3 to 5 weeks in Ullevål Hospital "too wild in the head, nervous". (Where did that come from?) "from too little sleep". Grown up in Kristiania [Oslo]. – Went to X School, graduated from 5th grade, had started 6th, but was put down again. (Why were you put down?) "I skived a bit" – did not attend forced schooling "have never been under the Care Services". When he rejoined the 5th grade it was in a class "with full benches". He "did not read much" as a boy – "skipped a lot of the reading of course". (Was learning easy or difficult for you?) "Well, depends how you see it of course." Has always been at Y shop as an adult. Has been arrested a couple of times for drunkenness – otherwise never been in an institution. About 19 years ago he saw – or believed he saw the late Mrs M. who owned the shop previously – he saw her when he went down in the cellar one winter's afternoon to fetch coal and she looked black, he grew frightened and ran back out, but soon returned to the cellar. He told people that he thought he had seen Mrs M. He has not thought about this since. (Do you think it was Mrs. M.?) "Oh, no."; he believes such visions are things that just come "which make your eyes black out" – "I do not believe in it" – he has not had other visions apart from the aforementioned. No voices. He heard a person say out in the street once, (he lives in 50 XX, 2nd floor) "Is this where he lives?" but it [the person's comment] wasn't about him. Physical and mental capacities have been intact – "and I have always been in good shape", but when he came here he "[got] a bit ill again – coming here from XX was something I didn't like". [. . .] He stresses that he went about brooding, over whether he was in the way, "had done anything wrong by the others" – (explain?) "– yes well, last time – I cut myself" (how?) "cut myself on my left wrist" – with a shaving knife – "that's what I regret doing so much." This was June nth, the same day that he arrived at XX.[32] Polite, rather childish. Depression with paranoid tendencies.

This Lab-investigation dates from around the same time as the previous one, but the patient's voice is reported differently. The parenthesised (polite), which forms an answer to the patient's question, shows a certain disinterested superiority in the writer from the outset.

The extract contains long sections of plain narrative, as for example the vision of Mrs. M. 19 years ago. The writer seems to favour the use of summarising passages in which sections that he finds interesting can be condensed. There is less of a feeling of a meeting between two equal voices.

---

32 We are informed earlier in this patient file of an attempted suicide.

This may be because of the patient's "childishness"; to assume equality with such a conversation partner is unlikely for the writer, nor does he indicate that he thinks it necessary. Nonetheless, the summarised sections consisting of plain narrative seem far more patient-friendly than what we are familiar with, probably because there is no attempt at subjugating the patient to the hospital's worldview.

The impression of the writer's relationship to the patient is entirely different in the Lab-investigation than in the subsequent short notes in the report:

> 11) Points out to the director that he is not a swine, which is the common assumption here.

> 12) Nurse reports the pt. is difficult and obstinate. A couple of times lately he has walked past the ward round without greeting them [. . .]

The hierarchy that seemed to have been suspended during the dialogue in the laboratory, continues large on the outside. In reporting that the patient ignores the doctors' round without saying hello, the writer turns our attention onto the hospital's wounded vanity.

The use of dialogue in the Lab-investigations forces the writer to mark the difference more clearly between his and the other person's speech. In the following fragment the quotation marks imply that the speech is the patient's "own" and is "accurately" recorded, while *simultaneously* creating a *distance* from the reliability of what is said.

> 13 (1916) Secretary 32 years. She explains herself willingly, is friendly and compliant, with a relaxed gaze. She says she has had a nervous disposition "forever".

The word "forever" appears to come straight from the patient's mouth, yet the use of quotation marks here, points to the possibility that the word should not be taken quite literally. This paradoxical use of quotation marks is common in all types of writing. This extract comes from early on in a Lab-investigation; whether the writer has already had any contradictory evidence to make him doubt the patient's word, we are never told. On the surface of it the laboratory conversation seems to be held on a relatively equal footing, and there is barely any evidence of the writer's past activities in relation to the case. The introductory and concluding remarks are given with absolute authority, without the writer referring to his own presence in the text. Whatever the writer posits has validity independent of the patient behind the statement.

Thus the Lab-investigation becomes a hybrid form: absolute authority mixed with absolute equality between two parties. The intimacy between doctor and patient is prominent; the conversation is real and takes place between just the two of them. But the equality is framed by an authority to which no reservation is attached. The patient therefore becomes extra visible in records with good "laboratory-dialogues"; the patient is allowed, for a brief moment, free reign in a textual space rarely afforded him elsewhere.

The record above continues with the Lab-investigation, which also makes extensive use of summaries, largely using free indirect speech, where in principle the voices of the narrator and patient become inseparable. It is obvious that if this form of discourse dominates (at the expense of direct speech), then one of the unique characteristics of this type of research becomes lost. But the following quote contains some further innovations in the reporting of the patient's voice.

> 14) Knows nothing about gossip or unfairness. "I have been worried about not doing my duty." When she last fell ill, she got the feeling that she wasn't quite herself, that she was tormenting those nearest to her and causing them all sorts of pain, that she had no feelings. When she went out with her mother, she felt she only "went along" – "I could just walk forever without aim . . . I did not feel the same as before . . ." "I felt I belonged nowhere" . . . "I had a sensation in my body, that things were not as before . . . so strange . . . not like a living being . . ." (didn't nature look the same to you?) "it left no impression . . . I could be joyful before, now I could feel joy at nothing." [. . .] "My life was gone". During this she felt despondent and found the days long. [. . .] (feelings towards family) "all love was gone, that was what was so dreadful." [. . .] Once, after 8 days without sleep she felt "so strange in the head and all my body, but I saw nothing else" (answer to a question on delusions) (after a few explanatory words on her sense of personality she explains) "It's as though I have changed, I am not the same as before" (Do you think that nature, people . . . have a different appearance) "No, it has been the same to look at, it's as though I'm different." "I feel that I don't belong anywhere" [. . .]

New in this text are the many consecutive lines of speech quoted from the patient without any record of the doctor's questions: each of the patient's statements is carefully bracketed by quotation marks, which "collide". We have already touched on the problems of the depiction of the patient's speech as continuous, when it is in fact prompted by questions that go unrecorded. Here we see that it is not just free indirect speech that is affected by a double voice; it is also a feature of continuous patient speech, which is directed by someone who remains silent in the text, yet active in the conversation.

In one of the Lab-investigations, the patient arrives for the session with a nurse as escort. The writer is faithful to the unspoken idea of an equal meeting between the patient and writer. The nurse's comments are *not* given greater validity. The nurse clarifies various issues, particularly in relation to the patient's sight and hearing problems. As soon as the patient interrupts, *her* speech is allowed to dominate the discourse, with no attempt from the writer to force a sane logic on the text.

15 (1925) (Lab.) She has a happy appearance, sits down – says "I have been in here for 1½ years . . ." The nurse, who has only known the patient briefly, says that for the last 14 days the pt. has lain in a corner both day and night, since she doesn't want to lie in her bed. The pt. interrupts at this point and states that she has been in hospitals for 5 years – additionally the nurse adds that the pt. is now calmer and less noisy than in the summer; she now sits doing handicraft work. Pt. interrupts and says that it makes her so nervous, that her husband is always chasing her and wants to kill her. [. . .] The pt. – according to the nurse – talks about her husband, [saying] that he wants to kill her, that the children are suffering. Pt. interrupts: "I hear them" – she sees them "so clearly before her", but when she reaches for them when she thinks "they are very close", they disappear like air, they wail and scream. Then, the nurse says that the pt. sees the parents of the nurses and how they look. Pt.: "I see so many dead" – "I see both the living and the dead" – she "cannot see the difference" between the dead and living. They buried her mother at XX Cemetery, now she sees her mother alive. Her mother was in her room at K., she says this was in April 1921 [. . .] (alone [illegible] with pt.) She has a friendly expression and talks willingly about her hallucinations (how long have you been here?) apparently 1½ years – she came by car "with her father" – she refers to the nurse, who just left. Then she speaks disjointedly about E., about an uncle S. Still, she knows the month and year, but not the date. "I was admitted to U, 22/11 1920 – I breast fed a child for two months. I came from South America . . . the child was alive in Rio . . ." When she came home after 9 months away at the hospital, she was given the wrong child. [. . .] (where are the children now?) "I don't know" – she says that somebody told her that they are in G. Street and have grown up. But "I believe

I have seen them chopped" – one day she saw J, "with a chopped off leg" [. . .] "They scream" – "scream for help, with all their might" Then she repeats that they were separated from their legs, beaten and [illegible] and then you would expect them to cry for help.

The writer has gone to extreme lengths to keep the patient's voice as autonomous as possible, despite the patient's need for help. In the ensuing years very little happens with the patient, despite all efforts. Ten years later the notes have grown shorter:

16) She is deteriorating steadily, looks terrible and unkempt, keeps tearing [her clothes], so that lately she has been wearing overalls – she tore these apart too yesterday. [. . .] *There is no sense to be had from her when conversation is attempted; usually, it just results in a hollow, noisy laughter and some disconnected words without meaning,* occasionally swearing. Her expression is usually vacantly silly and often angry. [italics added]

As we have seen, "no sense to be had from him/her" was a standard formula in the first period. Here, however, an attempt *is* made to get some sense from her. The rest of the patient's record seems – as in the case with the shop assistant – unrelated to any of the information which came out of the Lab conversation. The use of the Lab-investigation may have had its roots in the changes that were taking place in the perception of Dementia Praecox, and the growing belief that behind the dementia, patients had unused abilities.

BACK TO THE OLD

Some writers seem eager to conclude their reports with such phrases as "difficult", "no sense to be had from" or "silly", which invite an interpretation of "uninteresting object" or "not suited for anything other than being here".

In the following note we return to the usual mix of direct and indirect speech, with use of quotation marks for both. But the sheer joy of writing and the richness of detail is greater than usual here, and resembles the notes at the start of this chapter:

17 (1925) 20 years, farmer's son. On admission calm, came reading the bible as he stepped out of the automobile, continued reading as he walked through the

entrance, up through the yard and sat down reading in the waiting room, quite unaffected by his surroundings, nods when he is spoken to, but does not answer questions. He sits today with his fingers in his ears, yet he answers the questions loud and clear. The session moves at a snail's pace, but it does at least move; he has to turn his face towards the window, to look up at the sky before giving an answer. He knows the time and place. In answer to the question of why he had to come here, he says: "The Lord is inside the light, I lack nothing." At a more insistent question of why "he might nonetheless have come here"; he answers "Whom He loves He Chastises". – Dr. J. said that he had to come here, and he was [engaged] in such a battle, that he could not speak, it was Satan that was after him. Then he does not wish to give more answers. But when one asks if he did not manage this difficult task [illegible] since he had such excellent help, he beams and says "God was with me when I won" – when he looks up at the sky he is asking God for permission to answer; he does not see God, but hears him answer his questions. "God is good" he says, and when He gives permission for something, the pt. does it safely.

Perhaps the reason this note appears so intimate and patient-orientated – apart from its level of detail – is due to the writer allowing himself a discreet use of *humour*. This is partly expressed in a gentle remark aimed at the reader, and partly directed at the patient, "The session moves at a snail's pace, but it does at least move". This humorous remark is at least partly *inclusive* of the patient. "But when one asks if he did not manage this difficult task [. . .], since he had such excellent help, he beams and says 'God was with me when I won'." The writer permits himself a smile, but does not refer to himself. Nor does he use irony over the patient's head. Throughout the entire note the questions being put are reported concretely – but the writer does not identify himself directly as the questioner; "but when *one* asks . . ." This passage is surely reminds us of Hamsun's wish for a smile on the lips of the serious scientist. All in all, perhaps this text represents a model approach to narrative?

THE LIVELY NARRATOR

Around 1940 the writer's linguistic consciousness seems to have weakened again. The Lab-investigations had been careful to accentuate the difference between direct and indirect speech, and purely narrative text was clearly separated out. The following story from 1940 lacks any such attempt to report the patient's speech directly, although its narrator is lively enough:

18 (1940) Patient arrives at the assessment, polite and talkative. He says he feels completely well. The police brought him in, almost certainly because he has been in NN hospital twice, but he only stayed there for a short while, was discharged as healthy, to a sister in ZZ. It so happens that he's been going around selling various items, shaving things and toiletries, this is not allowed and they probably don't understand why he continues doing it when it isn't allowed. But he's got to make a living somehow.

There is a sense of intimacy with the patient in this text through the use of phrases such as "it so happens" and "they probably don't understand". The gap between the two voices is erased to such a degree that when we read in the next paragraph that "there's probably no use in repeating all this", we are equally willing to accept that the statement might come from a weary *writer*, as an exhausted *patient*:

19) Pt. came from a very poor home. He's had a hard time, that's for certain. Father was a drunkard. Father died when he was 6 yrs. The fact that they didn't have money has obviously affected the oldest of them, he says bitterly. He has 4 siblings [. . .] There's probably no use in repeating all this. He was sent away from he was 10 years until he was 15. He did not have it easy, it was work all day, from early morning 'till late at night. Once he was knocked unconscious in the potato fields by the manager's brother who [. . .] had a fit of insanity. He was jailed for stealing before he was 20, from then he was with a married woman who got a divorce for his sake. From 192x to 193x he had permanent employment in a shoe factory, but since then he has been unable to get work. He has looked after himself by selling things, and never needed Poor Relief. He has also travelled widely, lately around the whole country [describes the itinerary meticulously].

In the statement "He's had a hard time, that's for certain," the free indirect style is so strongly coloured by the patient's choice of words, that the statement could equally well be *direct speech* as *reported speech*. The writer does not use quotation marks, but nonetheless uses post-positioned speech markers such as; "he says bitterly". The text is undoubtedly heavily edited, but not so much that the reader ever loses sight of the patient.

There can be no doubt that this is a writer with his own peculiar narrative skills, and yet there is reason to assume that his storytelling style – straight forward but so coloured by the patient's speech that it sometimes dominates the text – is also representative of the period in which this text belongs. We have previously described this phenomenon as a spreading of the patient's linguistic zone so that it begins to steer the direction of the discourse. The Lab-investigations foregrounded the writer's consciousness at the micro-level. The writer grew extremely adept at recording the patient's voice and worldview. Here, the literary narrator takes over. Phrases like "he says bit-terly" reflect the language of the novel.

Further on in this record the same writer shows a command of, and affinity with, the clichés of the popular literature of his day, particularly in his use of expressions like *hardened criminals* and *met his evil destiny in a backstreet at Tøyen*:

> 20 (1940) He had got mixed up with a gang of hardened criminals, and once they had him in their grasp, he couldn't see a way out. "I was only a little lad". In the end they decided that he had to assault a man and rob him. They primed him first with a lot of liquor to stiffen him up. But when it came to it, he still couldn't do it. He thinks it is against his nature to be a criminal, and the fact that he has not broken the law in the sixteen years since the end of his last sentence, is proof enough of this.
>
> [. . .] But he met his evil destiny in a Tøyen backstreet in the shape of Mrs. J., who ran the grocery store. He repeats it several times over, that if he hadn't met her, he would never have ended up at O. or here. Mrs. J. was a lady close on 50, married to an alcoholic. She invited him in for dinner and soon a relationship grew between them. He didn't care for her a jot, but after a while he couldn't tear himself away. Meanwhile he continued a relationship with his fiancée, keeping her in the dark. "That was not a nice thing to do of course." He used a bogus name with Mrs J.

The narrator's thrill in telling his story does not prevent his ethical attitude from shining through. There is no trace of irony in the description of the patient not having broken the law, neither does the narrator address an implied reader who is the patient's social superior.

FOLLOW-UP NOTES

In this period we see follow-up notes being added to files for the first time, offering details about the subsequent life of the patient. Their inclusion seems sporadic and random; looking back I have not been able to ascer-tain any pattern that dictates which patients have been "followed up", nor when.

The follow-up notes may be seen as an indication of the hospital's willingness to show responsibility, to show concern for their patients beyond the hospital walls. These notes may have been used for research into relapses etc. In many of them, one simply observes an urge to round off a story, to say what happened next. This is a pre-modernist technique, which reflects both the belief in the whole individual, and that the narrated universe has coherence. The following quote concerns a patient 26 years after he was discharged as "improved":

> 21 (1933) Healthy and independent. There has not been anything worth noting about him. He married some time after returning home, *he and his wife got some money.* [italics added]

The conclusion that there has "not been anything worth noting" is in line with what has previously been discussed, that is, it is the bad news that is narrativised. But the overall progress of this patient goes beyond expectations. What is touching is that the writer not only mentions the patient's social success, but also his economic success. Perhaps there is an element of surprise in the writer's note; to judge by this file's introductory remarks, such a success story scarcely seemed likely:

> 22) [. . .] as a child he was well behaved, but was less able than his [brothers and sisters] [. . .] Was about to get engaged a few years ago but then his girlfriend died. Not prone to drink. [. . .]

"Not prone to drink" is a somewhat paradoxical phrase: it signals the patient's well-ordered life, despite his illness, but *also* the patient's *low social status*. People from the higher echelons of society with the same diagnosis are never referred to as potential alcoholics.

Reports rarely contain reflections on whether any improvement may be expected, nor retrospective reflections on why some patients were cured and others not. The writer does not want to set himself up for too great a fall, The following extract comes from a file which, from its first to its final note, covers huge distances as far as the patient's state of illness is concerned, but at no time is it possible to predict the outcome:

> 23 (1918) teacher, 24 yrs. Arrived today, emitted a few monotonous shrieks, settled down later [. . .] She does not answer questions [. . .] When one asks to look at her

eyes, she puts her fingers over them and starts to cry when one tries to take her hands away. She performs a number of monotonous movements with her lower jaw and lies mumbling to her self.

The use of the present tense in the physical descriptions lends them an immediacy and simultaneously makes them *continuous*. Possibly this is a leftover from the early Gaustad records. The use of present tense in such descriptions seems to carry on well into periods of psychiatric history, when the impression of the static nature of the situation would otherwise be played down. Half a year later, verbal contact with the patient is recorded:

24) She stands in the hallway today looking out through the window. Is friendly and cooperative, aware of time and place. [. . .] She is occupied with memories of what she has read. Talks about the insanity of Søren Kierkegaard's father and of the vagrant Peder Springer. On a couple of occasions, she has been dressed and outside. Her mood is variable. One moment she smiles and sings, the next she bursts into tears.

The sentence "She stands in the hallway today looking out through the window" has the same observational tone we see in the previous note. The situation is not commented upon, but one senses the ward rounds being done, the rush through the corridor. This observation is a passing "snapshot". The episode is intensified through the use of the present tense, but the writer responds to the patient's invitations to communication on the subject of Kierkegaard with silence. A little more than a year later the patient is discharged as "improved". The records have given no indication of how it was thought she might fare. Instead they give seemingly random, isolated, static images. It concludes with three short follow-up notes:

25) [. . .] was at home a bit [over]sensitive during the first period, later relaxed. She has an excellent reference for work completed as a supply teacher in 5th grade class.

Message from XX Hospital, that the pt.'s sister has been admitted there.

1934) She has been in work the whole time since getting well, capable of working, looks after herself.

It is hard to ascertain whether the follow-up notes are placed in the records for the purposes of shedding light on the previous entries, or if they are for use in any possible later admissions. There are no comments to indicate the intention behind these fragments. In the 1950s we will, however, see that the writers place a greater specific value on the post-discharge research.

INFORMATION FROM OUTSIDE THE HOSPITAL

The referral notes from the patient's district doctor serve as the starting point in patient records: "[. . .] from the admission papers given by district doctor NN, the following is entered [. . .]" Throughout the 1930s references are expanded and systematised to acknowledge the contributions of "others". For example; "[. . .] medical notes from Dr. H. based on pt. and his mother"; and later in the same file: "Pt.'s brother informs."

In a note from 1944 we find the doctor's initials *before* writing commences. The addition of initials is probably an indication that the era of absolute subjectivity is over: the subjectivity that was so sure of itself, that it presented itself as the opposite – as utterly objective and indisputable.

During the early 1950s, in particular, we see that people go to great lengths to seek out other sources to provide information about the patient. This surely reflects a desire in the period to re-find the faith we observed back in the 1890s, of being able to get a full picture of the patient, in which the patient was clearly one thing or another, and in which the validity of that complete portrait was unquestionable. But in this later period, the *opposite* route is taken: the "full" picture is constructed from a huge number of tiny fragments.

For example, we find meticulously made copies of various school reports received by the hospital, and even letters from former teachers about the patient's abilities, probably in connection with assessments of patients for lobotomies. However, the relevance of this information is *not* discussed until the 1970s. The documents merely sit there; their very existence in the records seems to be justification enough. Yet, when this information is simultaneously related back to a source – concrete and subjective – this also opens up for a non-objective understanding of the patient's world. Paradoxically this does not seem to present a problem for the writer.

The accumulation of unprocessed information is a trend in today's records too. Files brim with copious computer printouts of assessments. The patient files become encyclopaedic collections of knowledge, which nobody could begin to organise in any order of importance.

In the following note the external information concentrates on the patient in his social role. A note from a file that begins back in 1938 contains an entry concerning the patient's fourth hospital stay, in the 1950s. "Through the company doctor at NN Factory, contact has been made with one of the pt.'s work managers, CB, who has come to a conference today:"

> 26) Infmt. has known the patient since he started at the factory in '43. He has always taken an interest in the pt. because he has always been a dutiful and reliable worker so long as he is well – Pt. has however always had times when he seems "completely gone" [. . .] These attacks can last from 3 days up to a week, and the foreman has always tried to cover up the pt.'s strange behaviour by putting him on washing and clearing duty, where he can do things in his own way. Even in these bad periods the patient makes himself very useful, even though he works much slower than usual and often washes and tidies the same spot over and over again, he might for instance wash the toilet 5x in one day, when this is normally only done once a day. When these periods of distress have passed the foreman notices straight away since the pt. regains his relaxed and calm facial expressions, and can be immediately returned to his normal work on the conveyors, which he looks after better than most, for months at a time.

The hospital may collect information from a patient's schoolteacher to check if his/her cognitive ability is satisfactory, as part of the planning of further treatment. But the hospital may, as we have seen, also call on people from the world of work who want to help the patient to function better in his or her everyday activities. The content of this note is impressive: the foreman's easygoing friendliness, and the fact that his tolerance is not at the expense of productivity: "the foreman has always tried to cover up the pt.'s strange behaviour by putting him on washing and clearing duty, where he can do things in his own way. Even in these bad periods the patient makes himself very useful".

The hospital and the workplace discuss what can be done in the future:

> [. . .] Infmt. wishes to continue helping the patient in the future, but feels that he can no longer participate in piecework in the transport department. Infmt. is of the opinion that it must be possible to arrange a place for the pt., some clearing work or such, at the NN Factory where the pt. is not so dependent on cooperation

with the other employees as he is in his present job. Infmt. recommends that the hospital discusses this with the NN Factory management. The director does not apparently know about the irregularities that have taken place; [. . .] As long as Infmt. has known the pt. he has never been aggressive or involved in fights with his workmates. He is generally well liked, and the workers have also been tolerant of him during his bad patches.

In 100 years' worth of records it is natural that socially and historically specific details surface now and again. No matter the discursive format: the note above occasions immediate admiration for its openly expressed *workers solidarity.*

It is cause for reflection that the optimism we find in the records concerning some patients in the 1950s and 60s, revolves more around the *need for manpower*, which was high on the agenda in post-war Norway with its reconstruction requirements, and less around immediate psychiatric factors. Simultaneously, expectations of, for example, living standards were far more modest than those we are now used to. The result of this view of society can make it hard for a modern reader of these patient notes to see how the patient can manage "in the community" at all. Judging by the picture he draws of his patient, it seems clear that the writer is taken aback at neither the patient's job nor his type of accommodation, and lets it shine through that the patient's existence is perceived as being far from meaningless.

Most literary critics do not believe in a straight mirroring of literature and reality. But I have postulated precisely this; that economic conditions in Norwegian society in the 1950s and 60s led to a different kind of attitude to insanity which can be read – more or less directly – from the texts about them.

Another puzzle about history's place in patient records deserves a mention here: The above notwithstanding, one never sees the evidence of historical events in the patient files *directly*: throughout the entire Second World War, it is virtually impossible to find patient notes that refer to the war itself. On rare occasions one might find references such as "refused to go back to bed yesterday after the air raid siren" or "arrived in Oslo after the evacuation of Finnmark", but the references that deal with the war are always implicit and are assumed to be known; "the evacuation" is in the definite. These notes are written for their day.

One note tells of a patient, an elderly gentleman, who has had eight children. He cannot say how many of them are alive now. This would usually be significant psychiatrically speaking. In the notes in question, however, after bombing raids, evacuations and fleeing, it is a statement that principally says something about intersubjective relationships in a specific period of history. The less the writer is aware of his own historical position, the more difficult it will probably be for him to single out the psychiatrically most relevant information. The same problem would be applicable to patients from cultures other than our own.

THE SOCIAL MISFIT

The need for manpower coupled with increased tolerance can give patients greater opportunities outside the hospital. But when mental illness becomes associated so closely with *social function,* the pendulum can also swing in the opposite direction. The social misfit can suddenly risk being labelled as ill. The following note displays attitudes that are diametrically opposed to those in the previous example:

27 (1946) Reason for admission: His anxiety and vagrancy.

Here, the *psychiatric* state of anxiety is put on a par with *social* vagrancy. Again we are close to Foucault's theories in *Madness and Civilization;* where madness is used as a definition of those that fall outside society. We regularly find residues in our textual corpus of an attitude in which insanity is set up against a morally superior life, as defined by prevailing norms. We read, for example, of a nurse who is admitted around 1930, and who, echoing stereotypes from Gaustad's earliest days, has apparently "lived an abstemious and respectable life". It seems that some of the old, fixed phrases linger on in the patient records into periods where their content no longer has validity in other public spheres. The genre conventions survive. The psychiatric patient is assessed according to norms that society in general attaches little value to. This means that the assessment of patients (and potential patients) risks being conservative, old-fashioned and even reactionary.

This one-time vagrant becomes, 10 years after his discharge, the object of a proactive follow-up report. The following note is a study in tactlessness, and narratologically speaking it adds little. Here, the hospital's natural authority is tested outside its walls. These professionals are so blinded by their power that they do not, for a moment, worry about where the limit should go in wielding it: they turn up unannounced and make evaluations based on the norms of the hospital. Ten years after his stay at Gaustad, this person finds himself cast once more in the role of patient. Additionally, the writer is untroubled by referring to him throughout the report again as the *patient*:

> 28) 1956) follow-up study. The patient is met in BB's work barracks where he has his home. [. . .] The pt. says that he is quite content with his existence. In his spare time he stays mostly inside the work barracks. His main interest is reading and he rarely spends time with others. [. . .] The pt. is unwilling to talk about his illness, says initially that it all is so long ago that he doesn't remember anything, and besides he thinks it is unpleasant to stir up the past. [. . .] Pt. is friendly and cooperative during the conversation, but he seems far from relaxed. Emotionally he seems somewhat limited with poor capacity of emotional resonance.

The follow-up study has taken place at the hospital's instigation. The patient is quite content with his present existence, and nobody has asked for the man to be checked up on. The writer does not show the least sign of having considered the appropriateness of disturbing the man in his environment.

Ten years later, it is time for a new follow-up study. At an even later date, this man, who had been visited without his permission, expresses the damage that he suffered as a result of the hospital contacting him at his home: people who had previously known nothing, had got wind of his stay at Gaustad in the past. In the notes we see the worlds of the "writer" and "patient" clash; but it is the confined norms of the writer that prove unassailable and correct. The writer is unable to see that his subject has a changeable status.

> 29) follow-up study. [. . .] The hospital stays were a waste and he does not know if he needed to come to G. Some people have made spiteful remarks; after the last follow-up study others got to hear that he had been ill . . . [. . .] he is reluctant to talk about illness and symptoms, says it is very quiet in the barracks, closes the window when someone enters. *Does not seem suspicious otherwise*, is quite relaxed when he talks about his work and life at the barracks.
>
> His room shows evidence of his bachelor life, messy and not cleaned, laundry and unwashed cutlery, a large number of malt beer bottles. Denies using alcohol. Seems more like a loner than a schizophrenic. No grimacing, no conspicuous laughter. [italics added]

The man's very understandable precaution of closing the window – based on previous experiences – is turned into a psychiatric symptom: "Does not seem suspicious *otherwise* . . ."

There are further notes on this same patient from the 1960s and 70s, which throw light onto additional problems of patient follow-ups. It is still obvious that the writer finds it difficult to understand that the authority of the hospital does not extend beyond its walls:

> 30) He is not exactly thrilled about the follow-up studies from Gaustad in 1956 and 1966. It became known at his workplace that he had been admitted. He was distressed upon hearing about it all again.

The writer still gives no indication that he understands the situation of the person living back *outside* in society. A stay at Gaustad *is* socially stigmatising for this man, as it would be for anyone else in this period.[33]

It is puzzling that this writer – who, in fact, expressed extreme sensitivity to the patient when working previously in the Lab-investigations, has changed his attitude so completely when he is involved in his proactive research.

It must always be a great challenge for the writer to understand the restrictions inherent in the status of the patient. The patient role is something one enters into, and which one inhabits for a limited time, be it short or long. Even in cases where the outcome is fatal, the patient role is delimited in time. One is "delivered" back to society on the outside. During a funeral the ex-patient is again afforded social attributes that have, during hospitalisation, been absent.

This same patient record contains a note describing a patient/doctor meeting held in the different environment of the doctor's office. Here within the hospital's territory, the hospital's worldview is no longer placed above the patient's. The writer exhibits far greater understanding for the patient when he is on his own territory, and the following note may seem to confirm our previous claim that patient-understanding increases when medical authority is at its most absolute. Once again we are coming close to Foucault's thinking. But as we will see, this note is narratologically unique too:

---

33 Gyldendal's French-Norwegian dictionary had an entry for the word "Gaustad-kanditat" with "fou" given as its translation in editions as late as the 1970s.

31 (1971) Ambulant [. . .] Recently the patient wrote and wished to have a copy of all papers concerning his illness, since he was thinking about what the cause might be. Today he came by appointment for a conversation. [. . .] he says that in reality he doesn't care about any of it himself, but he has found the way follow-up studies have been carried out upsetting, since it somehow got out amongst his work colleagues that he had been admitted to Gaustad. It would have been better if he had been invited to come here for a conversation, he says. [. . .] Pt. spontaneously starts talking in some detail about the doomsday experiences he had in 1968. He had been relatively aware the whole time, but completely absorbed in fearful experiences and visions of the end of the world. These visions were colourless. It seemed to him that all life on earth was obliterated, and the last thing he saw was some ash that blew across a bare mountain. Strangely the whole thing ended in a colour vision. Then he saw a rectangle with a multicoloured radiating pattern, where the different sections were gradually lit up. It was incredibly beautiful. Pt. has not had an experience like it since. Pt. would like to know what one thinks about the kind of illness that he has, and it turns into a conversation of nearly 1½ hour. It appears the pt. gains satisfaction from it.

The use of free indirect style dominates here, but without the ironising double communication in which the writer marks his distance to the patient by using vocabulary which could not belong to the patient (*see* above, p. 32). The patient's words "incredibly beautiful" are doubted by nobody; not the writer, patient, nor reader. To get a closer understanding of what makes this last fragment stylistically unique we must return briefly to Gérard Genette's analytical models: Genette emphasises a separation between "who sees" and "who speaks" in the text. The traditional notion of a "point of view" mixes these two things. But when the "Point of view" in a text is discussed, it generally tends to coincide with the narrator's voice. The question of "who sees" opens possibilities for the description of various *focalisation angles; external* focalisation indicates that the "eye that sees" is placed outside the fictional universe. The long fragment above is governed, by contrast, by an *internal* focalisation. One perspective is maintained, namely that of the patient. The language of communication belongs to the writer, but he does not try to break the focalisation, or take over the passage. The writer "sees" together with the patient. The result is a text that seems more patient oriented.

In this last note there is no use of either the accurate speech reporting achieved so superbly in the Lab-investigations, nor does the writer give himself over to the literary clichés in which he occasionally indulged so enthusiastically during the 1930s and 40s. The Lab-investigation may have had its strength in its faithful recording of dialogue, while being simultaneously aware that the patient and writer inhabited two worlds that were generally mutually exclusive. This internal focalisation, however, marks the writer's willingness to enter the conceptual world of the patient. Unsurprisingly, we have reached the 1970s with this last psychiatric note. Its respect for the patient and interest in his delusions both seem specific to the period.

Incidentally, the writer logs a criticism of earlier notes: Why was the patient visited in his home, with no warning and without his having requested it? In other words, we see internal reflections in the patient records. This criticism is formulated by the patient, but reported directly by the writer, who finds no reason to take a stance to it.

THE CRITICAL PATIENT

In cases where the patient is what we might nowadays regard as resourceful and independent minded, it is possible to detect the hospital system's scepticism and concern about his or her becoming too involved in his own treatment. Encounters with intellectually capable people have in the past resulted in conversations held on an almost equal footing. Now, however, in the inter-war years, there seems to be an increased defensiveness, especially in the ward notes. In the following passage the patient is a nurse in civilian life, and is therefore well placed to critically evaluate the activities she finds herself surrounded by and subjected to. Regular battles break out:

> 32 (1935) More recently she has developed an arrogant attitude, there is no trace of her earlier jokiness. She takes it upon herself to be the one to launch criticism against, amongst other things, the "horror regime of the sisters, no other words can be used". She will "carry on pointing her finger" at all the "brutality" that takes place.

Once more the quotation marks perform a double function: Indicating the writer's accurate recording of the patient's speech, as well as his distance from its content. Later, the patient criticises "the use of radio sets" in a statement that is unassailable in its logic, based as it is on the hospital's own premises; the interpretation of the asylum patients' symptoms:

33) She opposes the presence of radio sets which [she feels] are a *hindrance to people being able to distinguish between imaginary and real voices* [italics added].

Reading this note now, I find myself giving her my wholehearted backing in her priceless attack on the evils of the radio. But the writer lacks both the willingness and ability to admit that the patient might, on her premises, have a point. The quote is taken from the same note in which she is accused of losing her sense of humour, and the opening verb is far from neutral; "opposes". Once again we are put in mind of Knut Hamsun: "I might give much to see the psychiatrist with a smile on his lips." In Hamsun's case, it was Professor Langfeldt who lacked any warmth, here the whole ward lacks the ability to engage in sympathetic communication. It seems that this patient uses irony or sarcasm quite consciously. But expressing a thing by saying its opposite – which is, of course, the mode of sarcasm – necessarily presents risks for a patient; after all, the patient is not the one who controls what is true or not true. Sarcasm may be used to create distance to the patient in the writer's notes, but, returning to Kristeva, the patient-doctor hierarchy is dependent on the absolute rule of symbolic language in the hospital's writing being unchallenged by the patient. Up until now, the patient's comment about the radios might have been taken as an expression of the patient's well-regarded "jokiness." But care is taken not to allow the language of the insane to infiltrate that of the hospital. This is the most plausible explanation for there being so few examples of internal focalisation in our material. Allowing the writer to "see" together with the patient, would also threaten the symbolic order.

The following copy of a brilliantly formulated letter from this same patient bears witness to the risks of a patient using humour in the world of the asylum. The facts she outlines in the letter concerning her discharge are all correct:

34) Dr. C told me that I was being discharged to ZZ Hospital [her former employer] and the state pension scheme from 15/8. So it can no longer be as a patient that I am still here. Is it as a nurse that I am continuing here, and are my food and lodgings my salary? If the salary is no better than this, I resign herewith. Your sincerely, Sister A (in jest only).

To be on the safe side, the patient has to add that the letter is "in jest only".

The pleasure one gets as a reader from the patient's sparkling sarcasm and humour is somewhat diminished when one senses her carefulness in demonstrating she is not insane. One gets a fleeting insight into what it means to be locked up.

We do occasionally find writers displaying similar reactions to those I have expressed here. Sometimes new and eager staff take a sudden interest in a patient, that the hospital has otherwise neglected or has a more negative attitude towards. These idealistic writers polemicise against the other medical staff, usually in vain and usually only for a short period. In the case above, I found myself slipping imaginatively into the role of heroic campaigner against the misconceptions of others; and *not* for no reason!

THE UNTREATABLE PATIENT

One psychiatric file, starting in 1936, gives the impression that the system fails to have any effect on the patient. We have seen sporadic examples of this before, but this is the first time it is expressed so openly; it becomes difficult not to view the patient with sympathy. We see here a Messiah-like person who has been at the asylum for years and whose behaviour is described in great detail for long periods, partly because he is sometimes suspected of simulating, but also because he never ceases to fascinate:

> 35 (1952) He still touches people's feet when he greets them. This includes not only the priest but also the doctors. But rarely any of the nurses. He prefers to stroke their hair.

> [. . .] He slides fairly quickly into typical schizophrenic incoherence, with manic language and stereotypical turns of phrase.

> [. . .] His entire being and way of speaking expresses a kind of ascetic patience and submission which is entirely consistent. The only thing he might get up to is to give staff a mild chastisement. One never sees any really active sense of guilt behind the mask.

> (1956) [Two initials at the discharge] Condition has remained unchanged. Patient has been a magnificent help on the ward, tireless and patient, kind and pious, and has had to be held back in his eagerness to work. He has run errands for staff and patients at Gaustad and performed his errands entirely correctly and

conscientiously [. . .] A place has now been found for him at L. He is discharged today into the private care of NN, as insane, not cured.

Similar notes from the 1990s dealing with borderline cases that the system cannot "get a hold on" also contain traces of the writer's suppressed frustration at the lack of control, as well as a constant desire to expose the patient's game and force the mask to drop. In our own time, however, the asylum no longer has the *independent life* it once had. The fact that the patient made himself useful was unquestionably beneficial. The hospital was not meant to be a place to stay. To a considerable degree the asylum tried to be self-sufficient in its daily requirements; the work done by patients could be meaningful in itself, and not always primarily as practice for something *else*. This also created the opportunity for the writer to give the patient the best of references, and appear sincere when he did so. The man above *was* a "magnificent help", even if incurably insane. Writers of today do not have this affirmative opportunity. Perhaps that is why they so often adopt such a moralising and insulted tone.

THE PATIENT'S UNUSED WRITING

This Messiah-like patient had his letters read in secret, before they were sent. "In his letter home he expresses a desire to go home – but he never bothers the doctor with it." Almost all the way up to our own time there are letters stapled to the patient records, penned by patients but clearly never sent to their intended recipients. Often these give a completely different impression of the patient than that expressed in the notes. I have not included these letters in my material, but have instead limited myself to instances where the writer has produced texts *about* their contents, or where copies of them have been transcribed into the file. The nurse in the note above is characterised as "an extreme graphomaniac" – and rather a lot of unsent letters are included in her file, but they are never commented upon, neither behind her back in the notes, nor in dialogue with her. Most of them are copied into the patient files, as is the example below:

36 (1935) The most dangerous type of treacherous mire exists where the egoistic moss grows, and its closely related species of meanness. The bog-bean leaf is realness. Wherever that grows one may walk safely out of danger of sinking mud. Skis that can carry one over sinking mud are skis of the strictest, bordering on the

ruthless, kind of sacrifice. Recipe for soap that washes away sludge: equal parts mercy and honest helpfulness, to which is preferably added a strong faith in the final victory of good. Sincerely A.

It would be unreasonable to expect the genre to legitimise the presence of everything it includes. The patient file is in many ways a *potential text*, a text which is dependent on what will happen in an unknown future. Factors that might seem insignificant in the past might be brought out and given significance at a later date. Perhaps the writer has a dream of solving the riddle of insanity.

The following rather intriguing list from another psychiatric file, is also a copy from the patient's own writing and is dated. The patient's original script was also attached to the record:

37 (1934) Wish list: Pfürsich Persegoss Apricots Peaches Bacoo bacao-tea Cha Epyluphechia Chamfer tree Chrysanthemum Spruce Pine Fitz Pin Yew tree Larch Cedar tree Cypress Poplar Lime tree Maple [unreadable] Beech Alder Blood beech Sycamore Boxwood White wood Larranza Orange Sinapel aples Apfell æpler epler Apal.

Someone has taken the bother of copying it down, just as I have 50 years later. Why did the writer do this? What was it used for? – and why am I doing it? And for what purpose did the patient write it?

5

Third period: 1950–80

The two parallel aims – that of charting the development of the genre and that of identifying the essential forms characteristic of patient notes – will dominate this chapter too. Once again, I will attempt close readings of a selection of fragments, with the aim of exposing messages that may not be immediately apparent or that might be contradictory, as well as simply highlighting texts that are "well" or "poorly" written, or which I feel are representative. On a more general level the textual extracts will also illustrate possible changes in the genre; tendencies that might wax or wane, in contrast or in conjunction with the time-specific attitudes in society that surface in the notes.

RELIGIOUS LANGUAGE

In the material of the 1890s I was struck by the use of *religious phrases and expressions*. Perhaps these were particularly fascinating to me because they are used so little today and have therefore recaptured some of their immediate meaning? In the 1890s these religious expressions were not exclusively a sign of religiosity or of true faith. When, for instance, a servant girl writes that "every day has its own pain, but it is all in God's hands" etc. then the religious component contributes to an accurate expression of her suffering. Religious language gave ordinary people tools to articulate difficult aspects of life, which in our own secularised society, 100 years later, we can only envy. The fact that this same servant girl's letters were never sent to their addressees is a chilling side to life in the asylum. What use is there in possessing language, when it does not reach its destination?

We have seen earlier how touching the phatic function can be in the notes, for example where the patient is asked the dates of the Punic Wars. In these, the addresser and addressee of the message are merely checking that the channel of communication is open between them – just as we might check a telephone line (hello! – Hello! – HELLO!). Within the parameters of the communication between the doctor and patient, the dates of the Punic Wars themselves had no referential content – however historically accurate they might otherwise be.

In letters written home by patients, it is the so-called *emotive* function that dominates. The sender uses the language to focus the message towards him/herself; communicating his/her own feelings. But the hospital has – without the sender's knowledge – removed one of the decisive elements in the communicative process, namely the receiver. There are many occasions in which the insane patient seems, to an outsider, aware that his/her communication is failing to reach anybody. The unsent letters, on the other hand, seem particularly tragic in retrospect, because the person is not acting insanely, but correctly and communicatively, and the situation is manipulated. What occurs is a kind of *tragic irony*, which could not have been lost on the hospital hierarchy of the day either. The expression "tragic irony" signifies that the audience knows more than the actor on stage, as when Electra embraces the urn with the ashes of her cremated brother, Orestes, and sobs, expressing her boundless grief. As an audience, we know the situation to be different; the urn is empty and Orestes alive. We are witnesses to the game played with a blind person, and the futility of their emotions.

These unsent letters often contain painful questions too, of the type, "why haven't you answered the letter I sent you? Is it maybe because . . ." As observers we know that the patient's struggle to find answers will be to no avail.

But religious language could also serve as a form of discourse that the record writer and patient had in common – to a greater degree than later. It was a language with which to seek (mutual) help. In the first part of the period 1950–80 the everyday religious references have long since gone. But a *socio-scientific jargon* has not yet penetrated the language of writer and patient. In the context of the asylum, religious language created some equality between the two parties in their communication, so long as neither of them belonged to the clergy.

The religious dimension in this third period no longer manifests itself as a *linguistic feature*, but as a *component at the level of content*. The following example is a typical post-war note:

> 1 (1946) [. . .] pt.'s situation as an adult: At 15 she arrived in Oslo and took a domestic job, at 16 she started an apprenticeship at XX, thereafter she had a job at YY factory. Splendid references from her employers. Everything she earned went to the Inland Mission. She travelled to different meetings to listen to all the lay-preachers that visited. She was bright, Christian, content and happy. Was betrothed to another Christian. Has suffered tremendous self-blame following coitus with her fiancée [sic]. She fell ill and was admitted to XX just as they were preparing for the wedding. Depressed from October 1944, religious musings. She has changed in this last year, becoming quiet, introvert and frequently dejected.

Of course, I don't think that the hostility of the Low Church towards sex can in itself lead to schizophrenia. But reading about the tremendous self-blame following intercourse with her fiancé, cannot help but make an impression in our time, when the term "fiancé[e]" has lost much social relevance. Knowing how to find freedom in one's life has never been easy, of course, but we can also see how time-specific the obstacles to a person's aspirations may be. The task facing today's writers must surely be to remember that such restrictive ideals are not necessarily a thing of the past. We must assume that our time is also subject to some cherished values, with equally destructive potential for some.

GENERALISATIONS AND THE AVERAGE PATIENT

During the first part of this third period, patients are allowed less of an individual voice. There may be several reasons for this: Firstly, there is a tendency to focus on the *average* patient at the cost of the *individual*. Secondly, patients seem to be more frightened of the consequences of their own speech. The following quote emphasises the observer's neutrality and his desire to generalise:

> 2 (1951) Pt. is a very typical, deeply lethargic schizophrenic. Hardly answers. The few answers one gets, consist of quiet and brief unintelligible mumblings.

It is new for a record to state that a patient is a *typical* schizophrenic. What we are used to, however, is that the writers often describes how a patient tells his story, before we are informed of its contents. Here the description of the "how" is developed still further:

> 3 (1948) She is a pycnic –talks with no reservation, but also without eagerness [. . .]

What is striking here is the implied correlation between the patient's physiognomy and her behaviour. Her method of telling is related back to this physiognomy; discreetly and with no causal conjunction, just as we saw earlier. But this additionally creates an expectation that the content itself is of lesser importance, and that it can nevertheless be read as a confirmation of her physical appearance.

Another stark example of this is found in a patient file in which even the *father* of a patient is physically assessed during a conversation. Meanwhile nobody finds it worth paying any attention to the referential *content* of this man's speech, that is, what he actually said:

> 4 (1951) [. . .] father of the pt. comes for a conversation today. He brings a parcel of books with him, several copies of XX which he distributes to various people. *He is a typical pycnic, somewhat hypomaniac, with a huge capacity for storytelling.* [italics added]

So undisputed is the asylum's faith in its discursive format, that it is applied outside the boundaries within which the hospital normally operates.[34] In the last chapter we saw examples of how within follow-up studies, carried out decades after the patient's discharge, the language of the hospital record continues to be used in the description of the ex-patient. The writer tries to win linguistic domination beyond the zone of his professional influence. In the quote above, an ordinary citizen, albeit a famous one, is described in psychiatric terms. And again the description of physiognomy overrides the actual content of what the patient's father says.

In the previous chapter, I emphasised that the writer was more prepared to understand the patient's worldview when post-discharge treatment took place *within* the physical territory of the hospital. This willingness to understand increased when his natural authority was not under threat. But

---

34 Interestingly, the man (the father) is one of the most prominent Norwegian authors of the time. The quote from the son's patient file is used in a biography about him.

we have also seen that writers have problems with patients that are less seriously ill; those who are alert to their surroundings. But that they can sometimes neutralise non-patients, beyond the hospital, by including them in the patient file discourse.

We have seen patients' stories being evaluated in relation to physiological characteristics. In this period, we now also see the various types of treatment that have come into being (e.g. electroshock treatment and lobotomies) adding an altogether new component to the notes. The patient's scepticism towards the writer now acquires a dimension unrelated to his/her illness. If *what is told* during conversations is to be assessed with a mind to possible electroshock, lobotomy or chemical treatments, and the patient does not want any of these therapies, then silence and deception becomes any patient's surest strategy.

In the following example we notice an extraordinarily lively depiction by a writer who seems to be rather pleased with himself – and who writes in the first person, something we have not previously seen used so consistently as in this example:

> 5 (1957) [. . .] Status at arrival at Gaustad Hospital: When I come in to greet her, she sits nicely dressed at the night table writing a letter to her husband. [. . .] She explains spontaneously that her husband is 20 years older than her. "He is small" *she says suddenly, and when I raise my eyebrows a little surprised, she adds:* "although he's not that small either". She explains that he is a big, bustling chap physically, but she has difficulties in explaining in what way he is small. It sounds almost as if she thinks he is small-minded and not very patient with her behaviour, full of criticism [. . .] "Can I say everything?" *she asks suddenly a little suspiciously.* It seems that she is holding some of her symptoms back. It is not possible at the moment to get her to say very much about her hallucinations, as she did at the clinic. She claims that she no longer hears the voices of people, other than those close by. [. . .] "I never hear anyone who is in another house." [italics added]

The writer emphasises how responsive the patient is to his initiatives: *"when I raise my eyebrows a little surprised, she adds . . ."* Once more, the dialogue shows a strong resemblance to literary models. It took time in literature too, to develop composite expressions that indicated the originator of the quote simultaneously to the manner in which it was said. In Norwegian literature, Jonas Lie develops the form almost into a parody towards the end of the 1880s, in what is called the impressionistic novel. The aim was to encapsulate as much of the moment as possible. Lie sometimes removed the descriptive verb, replacing it with expressions like "continuing with her knitting", "bringing in the tea" etc. as equivalents of "she said". The expressive verb above is far from that unusual, but points in the direction of wanting to capture the situation through the expansion of the dialogue markers. The expressive verbs belonging to the patient have been given adverbial additions like "spontaneously", "a little suspiciously" etc.

Like many others from around this time, this note displays a peculiar shift between activity and passivity. Enormous efforts are made in this period to map the earlier life of the patient. For instance school reports including the patient's grades are found in files. Yet, not even in this period is there any commentary on the delusions that the patients are, more or less willingly, made to talk about. Any material that has come about in dialogue with patients is left unused, whilst a search goes on behind the patients' back for something else. The fears expressed by patients at times seem, therefore, well founded. Why say anything, when what you say might result in an unwanted treatment? The same note continues:

> 6 (1957) Conversation with the patient in isolation ward: She seems tense [. . .] is probably scared of what consequences it [all the questions and investigations] might have on her treatment and stay. She fears shock treatment, does not care much for the medication either, she thinks she will be well if she gets rest and care and can go for walks.

So, we have come full circle! Despite the writer's determined efforts at coming close to the patient, the patient's speech ends in nothing more than a desire for the asylum to be precisely that – an asylum – a place that offers respite, care and a opportunity to take walks. This old ideal of an asylum, expressed so succinctly by this troubled patient, stands uncommented upon and unexplored by the writer, despite his procedural eagerness up to this point. Once more, it seems that the writer is most interested in presenting the *typical* aspects of this case, and as a consequence, the thoughts and feelings of the individual patient are of less interest.

The fragment below is representative of the relationship between the individual and the "average patient" in this period:

> 7 (1955) The patient was distant on arrival, only partially aware of surroundings, impossible to establish real contact with. She answered questions, but usually

slightly off centre to the questions, and then with long monologues. She lay staring absently up at the ceiling and reported what the Good Lord told her. Added, in a stereotypical way the phrase "the Good Lord says" to everything she said. She was very interested in the phenomena of splitting, the evil and the good half of the brain, the Devil and the Lord who spoke inside her etc. This stood out more than the depressive content, the accusation from the Lord that she was homosexual and should not be allowed to eat as a punishment. *After a few more electroshocks there was more clarity in her condition.* [italics added]

The last sentence has an *invocational* function. What the tangible improvements were, we are not told. The narrative up to this point stands like some unspecified textual body. It seems quantity is what matters here. Does the "clarity" brought about with the electroshock treatment, imply that everything that went before loses relevance? If this is the case, one can understand the writer's eagerness to cure the patient through the use of electroshock; one wants to be spared the fabrication of a lot of nonsense.

During the next admission the patient herself takes exception to the last treatment:

8) All doctors must write in all magazines against masturbation. *Dr. X gave me shocks, he didn't understand my soul and killed it.* He said I have a split in my brain. God says I am a witch. Have heard God's voice in my chest the whole. [italics added]

A *battle of competence* ensues, over who is right. The patient does not get heard. The patient file later stresses, after more electroshocks, unconditionally that she is no longer difficult but calm; the two cardinal virtues that have followed us all the way from the 1890s. Here they appear in 1950s vintage, with masturbation still a disturbing element in the system.

THE LOBOTOMISED PATIENT

It is not unthinkable that the notes of lobotomised patients show some underlying unease as to the validity of this drastic procedure. The writer overcomes his doubt, and regains control by cultivating an exaggerated disinterest towards anything but the general, as illustrated in the example above.

The entry below concerning a female lobotomised patient is strongly influenced by the social values of the 1950s. This is especially obvious, as we shall see later, in the depiction of marital relationships. Some time after the procedure we read:

> 9 (1950) She is very good at sewing, but is stubborn and obstinate.

Before the turn of the last century we saw an example of a woman who was good at work *but* fond of dancing. Again, we see an interesting connection between two sentences. Is sewing an activity, perhaps, which should promote meekness and mildness in the patient? How can one possibly be "stubborn and obstinate", when one is good at sewing?

The files of patients undergoing lobotomies, in my material, generally include confirmation of a considerable improvement after the operation. Yet an explicit cause and effect relationship between the operation and the improvement is never expressed in words; rather, the proximity of the two sentences suggests it, despite any lack of referential confirmation. Again we note that unequivocal formulations are avoided in the comments about treatment programmes:

> 10 (1950) After the operation she has not been unclean nor had fits of silly laughter.

> 11 (1950) On [the subject of] her sexual life she says her sexual drive is much reduced after the leucotomy. She has stopped masturbating completely.

However, this beneficial effect is short-lived. Things are soon as they were before, without the writer expressing any surprise at this. It is not in the remit of the patient record to evaluate the past: We read that she "is highly strung and giddy, talks a lot of nonsense", only months after her "uncleanliness and silliness" were deemed a thing of the past. Later the patient becomes difficult again. But the old system of grading patients down the alphabet is at work so promptly that we realise that the writer suspects the patient of simulating. It is cause for reflection that the effect of the very latest procedures (read: brain surgery) is so fragile that one falls back quite rapidly on the archetypal treatment regimes from the founding of the hospital when faced with difficulties:

> 12 (1950) For some time she has refused to go the sewing room, just sits on Ward B sewing. It is explained to her that patients on Ward B are assumed to be well

enough to attend the sewing room rather than sitting in the ward, and that she will therefore have to be moved to Ward C if she is unable to go to the sewing room. The next day she went willingly to the sewing room.

Again we see that the cause and effect relationship is not indicated directly: "The next day she went willingly to the sewing room." But the information in the note above has no purpose other than to make the reader assume a link. There is a quiet triumph expressed in having defeated the patient, yet the writer remains cautious: the agent remains impersonal "*it* is explained to her": the writer shows he has the linguistic upper hand – he is in control of the story. Science is faceless – everything that has to do with lobotomy is kept as linguistically quiet as possible. This is true too of other notes detailing the same procedure. But it also applies – importantly – to the period as a whole. This neutral, scientifically motivated discourse may simultaneously be mixed with basic middle class references: NN (the patient's sister) is "nicely dressed and gives clear, straightforward information". Again the connection between the woman's dress and her speech is striking. That her information is accurate is, it seems, already predicated by her being nicely dressed.

The notes on this lobotomised patient discuss her relationship with her husband, but very discreetly. The unspoken aim is to get the woman back with him. There is not the slightest indication of divorce being considered.

> 13) Her husband is in Oslo for the time being and visits her daily. She has grown very irritable, says that she does not like her husband, would prefer to have nothing to do with him.

The hospital seems to allow her indignation to reflect badly on her, rather than on anyone else. Her husband is invisibly present as a daily visitor for a period, although the notes show no sign of him being consulted on his opinion after the procedure has been performed. He is remotely present as someone vouching for the institution of marriage. He has no role beyond this. It is not the writer's task to reflect upon the couple's relationship, or question whether perhaps their problems might be due to more than just her illness. The patient notes in this period do not, to any significant degree, attempt to access the patient in his or her social context. Instead it is explained to her again, neutrally and authoritatively, the arrangements her husband is making:

14) She will try, she says, to go home and time will show if she manages to live with her husband. It has been clarified for her that it is often the case after brain surgery that sexual activity might not seem as difficult. Then she says, "she knows noth'n 'bout that" and that part of the reason for her coolness, is that she felt such disgust at the thought how, when he was at sea, her husband went with other women and had had gonorrhoea.

The quotation marks and the passing use of the patient's accent, signal the writer's distance to the patient. His discourse is not mixed with hers. The power hierarchy in the marriage and society at large is demonstrated the following way:

15) It has been explained to her that her husband has given permission for her to travel to, and to stay with an acquaintance in XX for a couple of weeks until her husband comes to take her home. She appears very happy and pleased at the prospect. She is discharged today. Insane but improved.

That "her husband has given permission for her" is possibly a legally correct formulation, on account of her insanity. Once more we see the same faith in authority as in the note of the woman who opposed electroshock. Here the husband takes over the authority function that the hospital otherwise maintains. And the story has a happy ending. Order is re-established – although one has had a difficult case to deal with. And the patient is pleased at the moment of being discharged.

The patient has had everything "clarified" and "explained to her" along the way, but there is no attempt to verify that the communication has been understood. The patient is uninteresting as a person, she is merely an object; yet the hospital has acted absolutely appropriately.

THE HOMOSEXUAL PATIENT

In the following example we note both the writer's and patient's lack of discursive options on the subject of homosexuality, at a time when Christine Jorgensen seemed to be the only public reference point.[35] In the following

35 In 1952, the 26-year-old Christine Jorgensen (1927–89) went through what is considered the world's first successful sex change operation, at the Rikshospital in Copenhagen. The operation was an international media event.

quote, there is a *metonymic shift*[36] from feeling homosexual, to the choice between being a man or a woman, and from there to the question of a sex-change. When an operation is eventually suggested, it seems brain surgery (lobotomy) is just as much of a possibility:

> 16 (1954) Says that he has felt sexual attraction towards individuals of the same sex, but does not want to say what type of men seem attractive to him. [. . .] During the entire conversation he displays enormous tension, despises himself, thinks such things are detestable, at the same time as obviously considering himself a homosexual, but does not want to acknowledge it. The only solution must be to have an operation, like Christine Jorgensen, or an operation on his brain, talks interestedly about such operations. Otherwise we cannot really help him.

The quote ends in free indirect speech and we must assume that the words are those of the patient, although the sentence could equally well be the writer's own: An operation is needed if we are to help him. This seems quite a good place for the note to end.

But the patient improves. The next note follows electroshock treatment, and shows how complex and contradictory sexuality is:

> 17) Condition has otherwise improved during treatment, he has not spoken much about his problems as regards homosexuality and the like, been more open and approachable.

He has improved and no longer talks about his sexuality, yet has, according to the writers, become more open. The patient has opened up by closing down. His silence about his concerns is interpreted as openness. Looking back one has to be fairly blind not to detect a paradox here. But the asylum is possibly so pleased with having its patients incorporated into the moral values of the larger society, that the paradox at a micro level is not visible in the homophobic context of the day.

At the very end of this record we read that a lobotomy was already on the cards when the patient was first admitted, something which has never been mentioned earlier. The endnote places the patient's sexuality within comprehensible remits:

---

36 Metonomy = contiguity, as opposed to metaphor = similarity. Metonymic relationships are based on a principle of association. In the example there is a conceptual shift, e.g. the associative link between the two types of surgical procedure.

> 18) Conclusion for 2nd stay: Not worked in the last six months, hypochondriacally nagging, restlessly irritable, partly depressed. Looks in the mirror and preens a lot –. Admitted with questions about leucotomy.

"Looks at himself in the mirror and preens a lot": this simplistic 1950s cliché of the homosexual male is taken from an interview with his father, who was concerned that his son bought expensive clothes, and that his hypochondria caused him to wash and look in the mirror too much. It is precisely because this is such a standard cliché that it acquires additional significance and is introduced as a general conclusion. We have seen similar examples of narrative structuring principles at work in other periods. The writer takes hold of a seemingly random episode from earlier in the text – and allows it to acquire additional significance by repeating it later. The writer has considerable freedom to develop such leitmotifs.

Fascinatingly, there are likely be similarly fixed formulas in every époque for personality descriptions, which the writer will honestly believe to be *taken straight from reality*, whilst readers from other epochs might detect their formulaic content.

The writer is as subject to the society's norms as the rest of the population, however much he believes his science puts him on another level. Barthes has shown, in his narrative theory, that there is no position outside and above the text being analysed. The demands of a scientific approach must therefore include an acceptance that it is impossible to occupy a neutral meta-level from whence our investigations take place, but that we always occupy a position of interference in relation to the text being analysed.

RECORDING SPEECH "AS IT REALLY IS"

In one note from this period even the pauses and breaks in the syntax are recorded. The writer's logic does not correct or elevate the incomprehensible into the sphere of comprehension. The rhythm of the patient's speech is made visible. As such the extract can be seen as an attempt to bring the semiotic field, in a Kristevan sense, into the scientific discourse:

> 19 (1951) When asked if she has smelled anything strange she says: "Yes, when I am filming and things, then I smell something strange." She cannot talk about how the filming is done, she says. "It isn't paper films, – but it's very, you know –": She

often emphasises her words during the conversation. "When I am in a film – then I am on the other side – that's what I feel –."

This is a technique seen more often in our own times, but we already observe the beginnings of its use in the 1950s.

Few writers in this period feel the need to mark the patient's speech with such precision. However, it is tempting – since we are on the subject of primary techniques again – to pause on two short fragments with interesting endings. In the first the patient is given the last word in direct speech:

> 20) Since the pt. arrived at the hospital she has improved. She does not hear the voices so often and not at all during the interview. She denies that other people can influence or read her thoughts. "I can't read their thoughts, so I don't suppose you can read mine either."

I have already expressed a fascination for fragments that give prominence to the patient's voice in their conclusion. In the above quote, the writer does not enter into any discussion, and thus leaves the possibility open that the patient may be right. In the next quote, however, where a patient expresses scepticism about the wonders of electroshock treatment, the writer allows a pseudo-quote to be followed by an attribution "she says", thereby bringing the fragment back within his sphere of control:

> 21 (1965) She seems to have less of an insight into her illness than prev. but is aware that she needs hospital treatment. However, she feels more apprehensive than before about her admit. especially because of the electroshocks, which she believes drain her disproportionately, they make her more lethargic, and her memory gets worse, *she says.* [italics added]

I would like to return to the example of the multiplication task (*see* p. 51) in which the writer makes a humorous comment – in a meta-commentary – to the effect that the patient deserves the last word: "The last round therefore goes to the patient, on that note it is probably wisest to conclude the session." In this later quote, the last word again goes to the patient: "they make her more lethargic, and her memory gets worse, *she says.*" Yet the content of the patent's speech is undermined: The first words of this quote could be plain narration or free indirect speech. If it were put into direct speech: "'I get more lethargic,' she says", no uncertainty would be attached to the patient's statement. The text would be a direct record of what she feels. But this pseudo-direct speech, in the third person followed by "she said" makes the content of her speech about her feelings, something that she is not allowed to have a qualified opinion about or linguistic control over – however ordered the utterance might seem.

Good writers can, with elegance, allow the patients' linguistic zones to get the upper hand. In the following extract, the sentences are coloured by the patient's speech; with the patient's East Norwegian dialect even recorded to some extent. This time, the dialect words are not put in inverted commas, as is generally done when a dialect or accent is used, thus stressing the *differentness* between patient and doctor. The writer here has no need to mark a linguistic distance between his own and the other person's voice, probably because the content is so far from himself that the reader is in no doubt where to draw the line between the two of them:

> 22) Is actually from South America he says – parents wandered wild in the woods there. He came here in a whale, before there was time and things – before we got the sun and the stars. It is not that long ago, really. Earlier it was semi-dark and people walked naked about the woods and couldn't talk much – but this is something you know already, for sure. Of course we've had harelipwars too, he says. [. . .] He denies having any religious ideas, no thoughts about doomsday, about fights between good and evil, about being Christ. He has seen and spoken to Jesus often, he says. He himself blasted a hole in the sky, so that we would have the sun. And Mount Ararat is in Mississippi, which he has seen often when he has flown over America. He has a grasp of time and place, would rather not be here, but does not seem too eager to be discharged either.

Any reservations about the story are non-existent; indeed the writer retells the narrative with great alacrity. However, a paradox opens up here, which we can probably recognise from the entire 100-year period: When the universe described is far removed from the writer, he can relate it with more enthusiasm and believability. But when the story comes closer to his own circumstances, the story meets with more resistance. In other words: *The teller will tell better the less he believes in the truth of the related story.* A paradox indeed; but we have seen several instances of this, as for example in the enthusiasm of the story about Baron von Meatball in the 1890s. Now, after narrating yet another strange tale, the writer concludes his note somewhat surprisingly:

23) He relates all this nonsense with the same calm voice and with an expression-less face.

Why has the writer bothered to write all this nonsense down? When the writer comes closer to dangerous topics like sexuality, he quickly becomes more cautious, more resistant and prefers to move towards silence.

PARADIGM SHIFTS TOWARDS OUR OWN TIMES?

In the 1960s we observe an increased tendency to detail the circumstances surrounding the encounter between doctor and patient. In the 1950s it was important to depict the physical framework of conversations, so that we have: "When I entered the room to say hello to the patient . . ." versus the passing snapshots that we saw so often in the preceding periods, for example: "She stands in the corridor looking out of the window and says . . .". The writer in the 1960s marks all attempts at establishing conversation and also draws *conclusions* from these attempts, as in the example below:

> 24 (1969) *It is impossible to get a coherent story from him. [. . .] In an attempt to speak in the office* he obediently enters and sits down. He answers questions without pausing for too long but is consistently dismissive and evasive. Q.ed where his job was, he says it was some place. How much he earned – he earned a bit. About the journey, after repeated qs; that it was a company, does not want to say where they journeyed to. *The more one goes into detail and comes closer to his illness and his dismissal, the more dismissive he becomes [. . .]* It is impossible to break through this barrier. *Nor does he volunteer anything spontaneously.* [italics added]

The *silence* of the patient has been made to *speak;* it leads to a conclusion. This recognition of a kind of system within silence is itself new. It can be viewed as an indicator of increased interest in understanding the patient's reality. To the writers of today this example may appear trivial, since it has been common to mark conversation's premises all the way up today, and can sometimes be even be more detailed in its application.

In the following note too, we can see an underlying concern for the character of the patient's delusions.

> 25 (1963) *After being teased out a little he admits* that other people see him as abnormal. He himself feels that he has been normal all the time. He then volunteers

some rather vague pronouncements about the subconscious and the noises coming from it, *by way of an answer to a question about voices.* Says that he first noticed in 1952–53 that Satan's power had sway over him. He makes it extremely clear that it is difficult for him to explain how this happened, but that there was definitely something that made an impact from outside. He feels that he has been able to withstand Satan's power, but noises from the sub-terrain have forced themselves up to him. It turns out that by sub-terrain he means the earth under the cottage in which he lives [. . .] It seems that he confuses sub-conscious and sub-terrain and he reports that he has made various provisions to counteract the influences from the sub-terrain. *The above comes up during a short conversation during the doctor's rounds* [italics added]

Much of the writer's attitude towards the narrative is directly communicated in this extract, revealing the text's ambition to communicate with somebody outside it. His text does not merely give a passive rendition of what has taken place. With phrases like "It turns out that by sub-terrain he means . . ." the writer enters a communication *process*. This stands in strong contrast with the note about the woman who was good at sewing but obstinate and who merely had the arrangements that were made for her, either "clarified" or "explained" to her.[37]

Towards the end of the 1960s the shift from a *static and unchanging* view, which we previously observed, to one of *process* is an important and marked transition in the patient record genre.

In the material from the early 1960s, in which the writer begins to problematise the discourse in his notes, one occasionally finds a writer with a heightened *investigative curiosity* that I cannot help but be charmed by. Or is it that I – just like the writers mentioned above – am in a more sympathetic story mode when the discourse does not concern factors too close to my own personality? In the following textual example it seems almost as though the patient has a hold on the writer, rather than the other way around:

26) (1962) His behaviour only becomes conspicuous when his problems are brought up. Then he becomes talkative, describes in a rather topsy-turvy fashion

---

37 I am, of course, aware that the differences I allude to here may be related to the degree of illness in the patient. All the same, I maintain that based on the material I have had at my disposal, a clear shift in the writing half way through this third period is discernable.

and with a fair amount of stereotyping his persecution at his workplace. This is usually accompanied by dramatic illustrations designed to show how he was hit and kicked, how people have spat in his food etc. *Some of these performances are little masterpieces* [. . .] He is on great form at the study clinic today. – He is generally stimulated by audiences. He seems noticeably happy and jolly during this, totally free of the irritation that might have been expected. Carefree, jokey, making fun. Not evasive although his performances are possibly a little less coherent than they should be, based on his linguistic capacity. [italics added]

From the beginning a distinction is made between conspicuous/non-conspicuous. The insane patient has "areas" within him that are more problematic than others, and the writer investigates the limits of where these start. It is unusual to see the patient's way of telling being praised so unreservedly (*"these performances are little masterpieces"*).

In a note from another similar file which includes detailed and fantastical stories, the writer does his utmost to distinguish between different types of information coming from reliable, unreliable and fictive informants. This is an approach to recording that writers have hitherto avoided getting entangled in. The writer's frustration below is understandable, albeit bordering on the comical:

27 (1972) It was hard to get any really precise idea of his paranoid delusions.

At last – more than 100 years after the founding of Gaustad Hospital – the writer allows for the description of delusions, but he immediately bemoans its problems. Admittedly, achieving a precise depiction cannot be easy; we can see how much easier it was when the formulaic "no sense to be had from him" represented a satisfactory attempt at communication.

When the writer goes far into reporting the patient's perception of reality, a more obvious separation between *reporting* and *evaluation* takes place:

28 (1969) During conversation today, patient is clear and compliant. He understands that he was totally run down before his admission, but he still does not have full awareness [into illness]. He has, as previously, a tendency to completely ignore the psychological side of his case [. . .] *I have the constant impression that* he has an unrealistic attitude to his own illness and situation. [italics added]

We have, up to now, occasionally seen the writer refer to himself as "I", but it is not until the 1960s that we find a writer refer to his "impression" of something. We are entering a period where the writer is far more prepared to explore the boundaries between the areas of the patient's personality that are affected, and those that are less affected by mental illness. At the same the writer is far more exposed than previously to the frustration of difficulty of doing this:

> 29) [. . . as a conclusion to a long note in same patient file]: *During the conversation one cannot bring anything out [in him], other than* that he has no insight into his admission, no awareness of his illness, he is negativistic and possibly dissimulating. [italics added]

The writer's wish to "bring out" something reveals a fresh energy in this period. This expression is, as far as I have observed, new. In the 1950s we often find remarks referring to patients' fears of "revealing themselves". How much of the patient's reticence was due to the illness itself, and how much could be blamed on the treatments on offer? Patients' silences in the past must, without doubt, have been born sometimes from fear of electroshock treatment or lobotomy. With the passing of time the writer becomes less representative for the hidden power that was so indisputably dominant in the past. But in the process, he gradually allows himself an increasingly negative attitude to the patient. In the file above, the writer's irritation grows in strength:

> 30 (1971) As on previous admissions he dismisses everything out of hand that has taken place before his admission, adopts a very arrogant attitude, is at times full of *well aimed spitefulness and pseudo-logical arguments, which he quite clearly takes great pleasure in.* [italics added]

The phrase *"well aimed spitefulness"* signals that the writer felt *targeted*. In other words, he is wounded; something that the writer has never allowed to surface in the text before. Previous rejections have been based on referential matters that do not concern the writer directly. Now that the emotions of the writer are given greater expression, his negative reactions also come through in the narrative more clearly.

In several of the patient files from the 1960s and 70s the patient's thought processes are reported in long sections, without the writer's addition of any distancing commentary. What strikes one, in the example below, is the writer's intense seriousness. He makes use of both indirect speech and free indirect speech, but is careful not to let the patient's own linguistic universe get the upper hand. The writer is also careful to mark the patient's attitude to what is told. The fragment is not dominated by internal focalisation, and yet the result is a text shared by both of them:

> 31 (1973) It turns out that the patient has constructed a logico-philosophical system which he uses to explain how his psychological and physical states are governed. The most central elements or organs in the system are made up of food, stomach, prostate and a higher encompassing structure (thought). *The whole thing seems meticulously + logically constructed, but without his intention being that it should be anatomically or physiologically correct. He says himself that it is totally symbolic in its intention.* The primary ideal is harmony. Whether harmony is achieved is dependent on whether the prostate is full or not. This is determined by access to food. What the patient thinks of as the prostate and the stomach, are respectively liquid (fluid) and firm. The liquid symbolises his father and the firmness his mother. Even though he admits to a mutual relationship between the stomach and prostate it seems that he attaches, subliminally or otherwise, greater importance to the stomach (mother) as this is directly dependent on food. The intake of nutrition is therefore determined by the mother. Based on this the pt. feels that his relationship to his mother becomes a negative one and that the reverse is true for his father. During one phase of the conversation the pt. was very concerned with the foetal position. [. . .] Pt. is interested in drawing and writing. When it comes to drawing, small cartoon series *seem most interesting.* They all show a clear progression. [italics added]

We looked at an entry from around 1900 that also aimed at writing down the patient's obsessive thought systems. However, in this it seemed that the writer's interest was more driven by a sense of curiosity, The notes seemed rather voyeuristic and reflected a static treatment situation, something entirely absent from this more recent note.

When the writer wants, without distancing himself from the illness, to express himself on a level removed from the patient's voice, we get notes as in the example below (from the same patient file). It is worth noting that we have now moved into the 1970s.

> 32 (1974) He remains unable to control his underlying impulses other than by on the one hand projecting them onto the world, and on the other becoming monomaniacally focused on control and order. *This is seen in the way* he constantly searches for the innermost essence of things, how everything around one should be controlled by use of theories and models, we also saw it in his tyrannical behaviour towards the staff and fellow patients in the early days. [. . .] These were, of course, obvious defence mechanisms aimed at preventing therapy from taking its course. His tyrannical behaviour was a strain on the ward. [italics added]

Such terms as *underlying impulses, projecting* or *defence mechanisms* have never appeared in previous notes. This text is so different that it represents a paradigm shift. Yet the *basic structure* of the note is still recognisable: The initial summarising conclusion, followed by examples that prove it: *"This is seen in the way he . . .".* That the "tyrannical behaviour" can be explained as an "obvious defence mechanism" indicates a patience and a strong belief in *progress, over time.* (Once upon a time people were simply "difficult".) It is incredible that so many of these psychoanalytical terms that already belong in everyday speech in this period, have not been employed more actively before. Is this perhaps due to a loyalty to the positivistic hegemony of earlier times? It is unusual for the writer to hold back from using linguistic and stylistic features from virtually every possible field.

The writer is no longer shy of saying "I", since his entry into the text is no longer problematic. He is also able to discuss his own position in a very different way than previously:

> 33) *My contribution is to tell him* that it is, of course, a good thing that he can communicate more of his inner life, and has better contact with his inner feelings, *but that together we need to have a goal that he can manage* within the framework of an ordinary work-life situation. For he says that he has not been able to work. [italics added]

This is the first time we see the idea of the professional and patient having to do something *together*. This formulation seems – against the background of previous files – groundbreaking; the doctor and patient decide together. *Yet* the expression gradually loses its direct significance. The statement *"we* have agreed" is often indistinguishable in its effect from "the *doctor* has decided", even if the writer may well experience the agreement as a mutual action. It can, however, also lead him to expressions of frustration, disappointment and anger when the other party (the patient) proves not to want to keep to what "we" have agreed. Thus the "we", which seems so "friendly" at the outset, can be a risky notion for the patient, holding, as it does, such a huge potential for failure.

At around this time we start to see comments about things that have gone wrong in the provision of treatment. I have never seen another note, in any period, so full of self-criticism as the one below. Such a thing is presumably possible, when we are working on the assumption that "we are *on a journey towards something different and better*". We note too the writer's quietly ironic attitude to his own writing ("*With the wonderful benefit of hindsight*"):

> 34 (1979) With the wonderful benefit of hindsight, it seems that the ordeal of communicating his experience of himself as an unworthy person, his ambivalent relationship to his father whom he experiences as negative and authoritarian, and also about himself, and his growing attachment to me, and of course the pharmacological and psychological effects of terminating his medication completely, has become too much to handle for his feeling of selfhood. [. . .] of course we want to continue to work so he can mature and develop in the direction of being able to take more responsibility for himself and his own life.
>
> [. . .] On account of the communication problems between personnel at XX it was probably not made sufficiently clear what should have been elementary in the treatment of such an acute psychotic phase of restlessness, that the patient needed to be kept in bed as much as possible, or at least in his room, with as little contact as possible with fellow patients and personnel, aside from a few – the least stimulus possible! Instead the patient was included in meetings, taken for walks, allowed to partake in mealtimes etc. This over-stimulation naturally contributed to maintaining his restlessness.

That fact that this note comes from a transitional time is apparent, not least from the fact that the writer admits that the staff have been too eager in relation to the patient. Again the question raised for me as an outsider is: Where does all this energy come from? An expression like "over-stimulation" has had little resonance before. We notice that an underlying assumption in the writer's discourse is the belief in the hospital as an asylum.

As we enter the 1970s we have seen a tendency towards a more psychoanalytic attitude to the patients, which surfaces in the files; both writer and reader engage closely with the patient's linguistic signals. At the same time the general optimism of the 1960s still stands firm.

As time goes on a more aggressive attitude comes to the fore. Attention starts to be drawn to the *broken promises* and *betrayal* on the part of the patients, often combined with a conclusion that things "cannot stay as they are". This is particularly striking since this is the same period in which we have seen the use of the inclusive "we" and the emphasis on finding solutions "together". It almost seems that the writer has tricked himself and his patient into a corner, which the writer is then desperate to get out of.

Reading and understanding patients' statements – including everyday ones – as *symbolic* was new in the 1970s. The note below may be representative. Here the patient's behaviour is explained and interpreted within a collective framework. One registers the writer's narrative pleasure at being able to follow the patient's logic in a modified linguistic form, so that to us as readers it becomes comprehensible. This in contrast to previous long literary entries in which the writer's logic and common sense was prime, and in which the words of the patient had less significance. What is strange, as previously mentioned, is that this kind symbolic analysis does not appear until around 1970:

> 35) There is however a group meeting the same day and that obviously becomes too threatening for T [surname]. The room is quite small, enclosed and people sit close to each other.

The writer does not use "we", but "people". "We" would appear too inclusive in such a note. "People" signals a form of neutral distance. The note continues:

> 36) His immediate reaction is that it is "cold" there, and to remedy the obvious human chill that he feels he puts on an extra jacket. When yet another patient arrives, it clearly becomes too much for him and he leaves. He then has to symbolise strongly and distorts his experience of the whole episode, and becomes preoccupied with coldness, icemen, snowmen and such things.

This is an example of how the writer interprets the patient's speech – not as something absolute, but something that exists within a certain *framework*. The writer's thinking in this example may perhaps lie closer to a structuralist approach. The relationships between individual elements are more important than the meaning of each component; the chill relates to the context in which the patient moves – and does not have currency as a general statement. This writer's willingness to identify levels of symbolism is impressive. For the sake of contrast here is a short note from the 1930s, in which behaviour that might otherwise be presumed incomprehensible is rendered comprehensible:

> 37 (1935) Wanted the doctor on duty to take a walk with her yesterday, when he declined on account of being married, she flung the contents of her coffee cup in his face. Today she is in excellent humour, laughs, chatters and talks about the event yesterday, which amuses her a lot. She thought the excuse he came up with was silly, it would not have bothered her to go for a walk with a married man.

This extract goes beyond being a mere fragment since it almost stands as a complete short story. One of the genre's main criteria is that a seemingly random event – here the emptying the contents of a coffee cup – is put in a larger comprehensive framework. The note is strictly constructed in terms of cause and effect, with a clear conclusion at the end. Nothing in the story lacks function in the totality. The logic of the story is unquestionably that of the *writer*. Where would *the patient* have started and finished this fragment? The writer is careful not to attempt to enter the world of the other.

We have seen an increased interest in symbolic interpretations, combined with a willingness to offer treatment. But the writer in this period is also generous enough to *let things ride*:

> 38 (1977) We have agreed to adopt a careful approach with TT [forename and surname] *and to try to build up a relationship of trust so that he experiences the hospital as a place of refuge and an asylum to which he can withdraw when things get too difficult for him.* It seems too as if he is coming round to seeing us, and using us, that way. We therefore do not have any particular therapeutic ambitions beyond this. [italics added]

How nice it would have been if the patient's notes had finished at this image of a harmonious, cooperative relationship between doctor and patient. But the image of the asylum as a refuge proves to be fleeting. Ten years later the ideology will have changed.

The above note shows a great desire for symbolic interpretation. But further on, the same patient file *also* displays impoliteness and stupidity, with their associated attack on human dignity:

> 39 (1978) He is a very fragile, immature person with poor control of impulses and a fear of emotional contact with others. [. . .] *The tiniest thing can provoke him, for example if people disturb him when he is in the middle of listening to music, or if they enter his room without knocking or they remove his food tray from his table before he has finished eating.* It seems though, that things are fine if one respects his independence, prepares him in advance for what one intends to do, and asks him if this is OK. [italics added]

All the correct terminology is present, the interpretations of the patient's delusions are thorough and relevant elsewhere in the patient's file, and we see an appreciation of the role of the hospital as an asylum. But this can come to nothing when not even the simplest rules for human inter-action are adhered to. How different this note seems compared to the short text about the woman who tore her hat and umbrella to pieces; the writer had no control over her insanity, but reported the patient's reac-tion in a way that for the reader made sense, over the head of the patient perhaps, but still in such a way that both writer and reader gained respect for the difficulties of enduring such an illness. Annoyance at having one's food taken away before one has finished eating, or at people entering ones room without knocking are normal reactions. The writer's inability to see this can only serve to illustrate the writer's complete lack of basic manners.

Milan Kundera comes to mind here; according to him the most impor-tant discovery of the nineteenth century was not made by the great scientists, but rather by the author Flaubert, who showed that stupidity does not fall away with scientific or technological progress, but moves instead in parallel with it; stupidity is constant and will always find new forms of expression.

From this same patient file, with its contradictory messages, it is clear that the hospital has *time* at its disposal, as it also had – perhaps scarily so – in earlier periods. This file lacks the aggression and indignation that is often part of the writing in our own time when a treatment programme fails. This patient file has a note from 1984, which is unique in its calm-ness, bearing in mind that the treatment is failing to produce the desired effect. Never did the early patients of Gaustad have such hopes (with their consequent disappointments) pinned on them. In the following note the writer accepts that the outcome was not what he wished for, yet does *not* blame the patient:

> 40 (1984) [transfer note] He himself expresses that he wants a more calm hospital existence, where there are no particular demands for activities with an eye to rehabilitation, but which offers some opportunities for a certain degree of autonomy and attention to his care needs.

Occasionally we find snippets of humour in the records from the 1970s. As a narrative technique humour has been rarely used, perhaps because it was so sternly warned against in the early days of Gaustad:

> 41 (1969) During the evening however, she had a revelation which centred on the fact that Jesus had returned to Earth in the shape of S [her previous employer]. [. . .] On the tram which was going in the direction of her home, she got off at T. She followed a young bearded man, whom she believed to be Jesus. It was, however, not him, and since the last tram had already gone, she had to take a cab home.

It is hard to imagine that the word "however" was used by the patient. The discursive form is free indirect style, but the narrator's colouring of text uses a higher register than we would expect from the patient. This gives some of the ironic effect that Flaubert, as mentioned earlier, makes so famous in Madame Bovary; the person is endowed with a vocabulary which, at a given point, she does not possess.

In the same patient file, some years later, we find several notes in which the narrative attitude seems more or less the same, despite belonging to the period where symbolic interpretation has become the norm:

> 42 (1975) Pt. came a few days ago and reported that she wanted to announce who she really was. She then announced that she was the "angel of the world". This aside, pt. has fulfilled her earthly tasks in a satisfactory manner and is skilled and helpful on the ward.

So far, we have generally presumed that individual writers have, on the whole, acquired their way of writing from the contemporaneous files that surround them; that the *synchronous* aspect is strongest. But we see here that the writer mimics the narrative attitude of earlier notes in the file. Individual patient notes are sometimes governed by the patterns set up by a writer at the beginning: the writer attempts to create a holistic impression despite the fragmented distribution of notes over time. He continues the file without breaking with earlier registers.

OUT FROM THE SHADOWS

In a patient file from the 1950s we found the formulation "a very typical, deeply lethargic, schizophrenic" – in which we interpreted the writer's use of "typical" as an attempt at objectivising his scientific discourse. The fact that the patient's symptoms were "*very* typical" probably also made the patient "*very* suitable" for a lobotomy, the formulation thus helping to make it easier to decide in favour of the procedure. From such unhopeful beginnings this patient record goes on to chart a massive improvement, only to be followed by a matching decline back to its starting point.

The patient was lobotomised in 1953. After 20 years during which very little information is supplied in his notes, a fresh rhetoric breaks through with full force and optimism at the beginning of the 1970s.

> 43 (1971) It must be possible using a more structured programme, to help him function more adequately.

Beneath all the usual jargon about programmes, structures or patient's functioning, we see here a genuine desire to help and a belief that there must be some solution; "something must be possible". Aside from its purely rhetorical aspect, this note is one of several in the material in which a patient in the crowd is suddenly discovered by some member of staff, and in which we see a flurry of interest, temporarily, at least. A year later we find a triumphant note about the success achieved:

> 44 (1972) He shows great interest in the music evenings every Friday. Usually it is difficult to engage him in activities, but he goes every time with other pt.s to the music rehearsal. He plays a bit of piano and sings. He does not have such angry spells on the ward and he has stopped spitting. He sits with the other patients during meal times, helps himself and butters his own sandwiches. He often goes on errands for the ward and he is very reliable.

This improvement does not, however, last long. Gradually the notes about him grow more sparing, until things have returned to the way they were:

45 (197X) He is a deeply lethargic, lobotomised schizophrenic care patient.

We are back to square one, though no longer with the formulation "very typical", which gave the writer in the last period a certain sense of triumph at being involved in such a neatly representative case. About the greatest tragedies, however, the files remain *tacit*. "The rest is silence."

6

Fourth period: our own time

TEXT AND REALITY

Two years after I had worked my way through the initial patient file corpus, I was finally reading notes from my own time; covering the period from 1980 to the beginning of the 1990s.[38] The extra-textual reality grew increasingly tangible. The closeness I felt to these texts was as much due to their form as their content. I now shared, to a greater extent than with earlier records, the idiolect of the writing. I have already commented on the illusion of thinking that one can stand completely outside the text that one is analysing. Awareness of this problem is essential, particularly when one imagines one has established an absolute distance between oneself and the object of study. But now, with the writer and notes being so close to my own time, the problem is reversed: How to establish a position at sufficient distance from things that seem so familiar, that they are a priori a part of my own discourse?

Occasionally, files belonging to this final period described patients still in treatment as I had their records in my hands. If the name made me suspect there might be any reference to people or matters with which I might have a connection, I chose other files. But the shyness towards the texts and shame at my own voyeurism that I had felt in the early days of my research, made their presence felt again. No matter my precautions: the suffering described in the patient records suddenly became a physical presence. The patients I met in Gaustad on a daily basis, in the canteen or walking around the hospital and its grounds, were no longer at a safe distance from the records

---

38 To preserve anonymity in this chapter the entry years will be omitted.

I read. The relationship between writing and reality took on a new, non-theoretical dimension. The stories themselves became more important than the method of their telling – necessarily affecting my analysis of them.

The absence of historical distance blunted my analytical eagerness. When the medical-histories became too uncomfortable, I grew more fearful of the text and my interest waned.

But the problem I am presenting here as "mine", tells us something too, I think, about the impotence the *writer* must always have felt. Physically he also lacked the distance in *time and space* which is probably a precondition for any act of confession through writing, that is, to discover in writing something about the illness and make decisions about the treatment. These records have always risked being little more than a mechanistic *report*, with a certain *ritualistic* tint; set rules are followed, and through the writing of standardised clichés the writer may gain a certain cathartic satisfaction – even if extremely limited – of having "done all that could be done".

Faced with the material of patients from our own time, I rapidly found myself in a state of indignation, fury and powerlessness in the face of "poor treatment", much as other amateurs who, on the basis of having read a body of medical records, denounce the state of the mental health services. Yet the writers of these records, and those professionals who take it upon themselves to read them, must presumably go through a similar range of emotions in their work. And only rarely have they used the opportunity to write down their complex reactions.

The text's apparent shortcomings in addressing the urgency of the reality itself is an intractable problem. But having finally managed to get the time-consuming transcribing of patient files behind me, and having gained some distance from the texts, I discovered that today's notes can have, no less frequently than in the past, a subtext that conflicts with their original intended message, or that strays into areas beyond their remit.

These last files are extremely voluminous, with a great deal of space devoted to the individual story. And they are, at first glance, both well ordered and well formulated. Yet on closer reading this impression is challenged; logical and linguistic inconsistencies are now hidden behind the neat layout of computer technology.

It is difficult to present the information in this chapter with great linearity, partly for the reasons outlined above; a respect for the people makes me less inclined to expose the workings of the texts. Additionally, in this material, there are records of treatments having been carried out that I doubt (and

I am not alone in this) are acceptable under current Norwegian legislation. We will also see examples of notes that empathise more with the patient's world than ever before.

GROWTH AND FALL

There seems to be a shift in the material from the end of the 1980s, which goes from viewing the patient's treatment on a long-term basis, to the notes of today, which may seem more fragmented and lacking in any comprehensive approach to further treatment. Whether we would find this trend replicated in a larger corpus is impossible to say, but the following example illustrates this development. This patient file also shows the genre's most sympathetic as well as unsympathetic sides:

> 1) In sum his condition seems to have stabilised, the patient has settled on the ward. It is presumed that the psychological growth and maturing already taking place, might result in considerable improvement within the year perhaps. Therapeutic measures, especially psychotherapy, must however be provided with care and follow a thorough and competent evaluation if new, dramatic psychotic destabilising is to be avoided, or at least tempered.

Where does the optimism in expressions like "the psychological growth and maturing already taking place" come from? To what extent is the expression a leftover from attitudes to schizophrenia of the 1970s and 80s, and to what extent is it an adequate description of this specific patient's situation?

Some years later there is nothing left of the interest shown in growth and maturing. Following various admissions and discharges, patience is running low:

> 2) Every time his [alcohol] abuse has been discovered the patient has been taken aside by the consultant or ward staff. He is not prepared to consider whether he is trying to tell us something with his abuse. He stresses forcefully that it is quite reasonable for a grown man of 30 to enjoy a beer when he wants to.

There is still a drive to interpret the symptoms, even when the patient is refusing to cooperate: "whether he is trying to *tell us something* with his abuse" is a formulation I feel primarily belongs to the 1970s. But he is, of course, "not prepared" to do this.

The attitude towards this patient hardens. It seems increasingly clear from his file that this is a man that the hospital staff – alias "we" – do not like. Finally the patient – after having been blacklisted by all the town's hospices and hotels – is given a more or less permanent place at a care home, but this rapidly becomes problematic too:

> 3) It turned into a conversation around the importance of structures and clear boundaries and about consequences of breaking agreements. Perhaps it is easy to be a patient here when the world outside feels difficult. One of our challenges is to get him over on the active side. Showing responsibility. In overestimating his own capabilities he ensures his continued stay here. It is important that the patient gets more involved. That he is forced to come up with his own suggestions.

"Perhaps it is easy to be a patient here when the world outside feels difficult." This sentence can hardly be seen as plain narrative discourse, since it comes out of a conversational context. It is perhaps closest to a free indirect style. The referential content of the sentence is in itself the perfect articulation of the asylum ideal, yet it is put into the mouth, at least in part, of a patient who has proved himself below the required moral standards. The sender and receiver, however, are at the same ideological level. The statement acquires an undertone of irony – behind the patient's back: "Perhaps you think it's good to be in a cushy place like Gaustad. But that really isn't the intention." Thus the sentence expresses the writer's rejection of the idea of the hospital as an asylum.

The writer's semantic field is saturated by key words like "boundaries", "responsibility" and "consequence" to such an extent that the reality of the patient falls by the wayside, and the writing begins to show cracks in the form of paradoxical claims. Being "forced" to volunteer suggestions is a contradiction that would make anybody unhappy.

Later the patient is moved to a care home, but the home cannot cope with the patient either:

> 4) Outpatient note (social worker NN) Visit at SS care home [. . .] The background to this visit – repeated telephone calls expressing problems with the patient in the care home [. . .] The patient's own wish is to come back to town because, in his view, he doesn't get on in the countryside. The aim of our visit is to play for time, to have the patient stay a little longer at SS care home. As of today, there is no immediate solution to the problems of his living quarters and admission. During

the conversation the patient shows no awareness of the difficulties he would have in living and being in town [. . .] He still sees Gaustad as a good alternative, as a place to be for him.

The writer tells us that the patient does not "in his [the patient's] view" get on in the countryside. Yet the *care home* has also made it clear that he doesn't fit in at the home, which the patient applies metonymically to the entire countryside. There is, then, a large degree of agreement between the care home and the patient: in the language of the playground this is *two against one*. But the hospital notes, again in the language of the playground, *are cheating*: the patient's opinion is undermined by the words "in his view". Thus the writer manoeuvres the patient into the minority position; the text suggests it is the patient who is "one against two", and leaves him standing against hospital and the care home.

The main aim of the hospital is, in its barefaced honesty, "to play for time". I have not come across anything like this before; it could be borrowed from a crime story. A criminal under pursuit plays for time. The hospital's aim, which was once "to encourage psychological growth" in this patient, is now reduced to "playing for time" – and not for the sake of *patient*, but for the hospital.

The note puts emphasis on the patient's lack of awareness of his difficulties; but to the outside reader, it is the hospital's lack of organisation in finding a place for him to live that is striking. There is a letter in the patient file from a family member who, writing in the capacity of a lawyer, makes it clear that the hospital's conduct is in breach of Norwegian law on mental health provisions. An entry in the patient notes reads; "letter from family member is included in the file". Beyond this entry, the letter is never mentioned again. Is the hospital concerned about a possible court case? The writing sits in silence. Perhaps the sender gets an answer, perhaps the letter will form part of the hospital's collective forgetting. So many letters have over the years simply been placed in the patient files.

I find this patient file particularly upsetting because it is so obvious that the hospital's disappointment at not making the patient any better, combined with frustration over shortages in possibilities of treatment, results in a distancing from him. Throughout the whole material there have been files in which the patient and hospital staff have grown further and further apart, but the distance can seem even greater in notes from our own time, which so frequently make use of words and expressions that assume a communication between two equal parties.

INTERNAL DISCUSSION

From the end of the 1970s we find that the diagnosis is sometimes *discussed* in notes. In the following example the writer seems almost to *relish* the opportunity to debate various possibilities, before settling on a diagnosis. He does not even baulk at presenting the diagnosis as a question:

> 5) His ability to make contact as well as to seek it out is clearly better than usually seen in schizophrenics. He has not got the familiar black-and-white mindset and splitting which is typical for borderline patients. [. . .] *Should we call it a deep depressive neurosis, bordering on psychosis with a great danger of psychotic outbursts?* It should be noted that the patient's mental defences are not strong and that, in other words, he must be seen as having a weak self. [italics added]

The note still tries to locate the typical, but the typical is now something to reflect upon, in contrast to what we saw in the 1950s, where the pycnic's exuberance was so "typical", that the content of what was said was of no interest.

This opening up for discussion in the notes grows more serious when two substantially opposing opinions clash, as in the example below. The discussion relates to a transfer; this is a constantly recurring motif in this period, although it is rare for discussions to break out openly within the patient notes. Evaluations that are made, and any doubts that are expressed ("maybe pt. could be moved to . . ."), are normally expressed in a single voice. In this example a lot of space and time is spent before a final authority is brought to bear. And it is not difficult to see how the locum is put in his place by the consultant. Initially the patient's presence on the ward is justified:

> 6) During her first period on the ward the patient has been very reserved. She barely answered when prompted. We had to check continuously that she did not go to bed. She often sat in a corner by herself laughing for no apparent reason. [. . .] After medication her condition has slowly improved, so that she now participates in the physical exercises and we have better contact with her. However, she probably needs a few more weeks on the ward.

The note is calm in tone. The patient needs to be there; implicit here is the fundamental ideal of the asylum. Yet, in the middle of the extract a few sentences break with the norm in the quote. The passage marked [. . .] above reads:

> 7) There was a striking difference between her behaviour towards us on the ward and in the conversations she had on the telephone mostly with her son. During these conversations she seemed strikingly competent in her responses, asking clear questions and answering in a seemingly coherent manner.

Why tell us this? Is this detail meant to suggest that the patient is simulating? Or to suggest that if she were to be sent home, it would be to somebody with whom she behaves in an orderly manner? If so, then the writer has set up a convenient paradox that can justify a potential discharge, even if the patient does "probably need" a few more weeks on the ward.

Some days later we read:

> 8) Patient note (locum). Because of shortage of space at the ZZ ward, application was made for patient to be transferred from there to XX [. . .] The patient had arrived psychotic. During a short conversation psychotic traits were not apparent. Patient herself did not wish to move and it was not problematic for her to remain in the closed ward. Most of all she wanted to go home. The patient considered herself well and did not signal any motivation for treatment. It is not likely that she would have any therapeutic gain by being moved to XX. It is possible that a move might have negative effect in this phase, as she is stabilising following the last psychosis-admission. Application for transfer was therefore turned down.

The opening sentence is a standard formulation, which does not prepare the reader for anything unusual. After an application we might normally expect to find a note about the transfer having taken place. But here the application is assessed against any possible *"therapeutic gain"*, and *is turned down*. Who is it that dares to allow therapeutic gain as the guiding principle on which treatments shall be assessed in the future? The writer's negative attitude to the transfer is not left unopposed. A week later, the consultant intervenes:

> 9) patient note (consultant NN) Today patient is transferred to XX following reassessment. She is not very pleased at having to move as she says she now feels safe in our ward. However, she accepts the situation.

The writer finds it unnecessary to include details of what the reassessment comprised; the evaluative criteria remain hidden in the text, whilst there is no room for doubt about their accuracy. The consultant brings the writing back on track again. The patient's statement that she feels safe on the ward is left to stand as her own evaluation. The final sentence harmonises the conflicting sentiments. It almost seems reminiscent of a period before the introduction of medication: the writer does not indicate any other possibility for the patient other than to "accept the situation", but at least the hospital is spared the possibility of the patient becoming "difficult".

The note again continues with the writer's suggestion that the patient might be better than one thinks:

> 10) It is striking in talking with the patient that if one takes a little time with her, her level of contact and her ability to make agreements and assess relationships are far better than one might initially think.

It seems likely that this is also part of the strategy to dislodge her connection with the hospital. The writer's attitude contains a kind of amazement at the patient, who is perhaps playing a game with the hospital staff. Strategically, this part of the text fragment reaps huge rewards, seen from the perspective of an over-stretched hospital. The logic being; that since the patient is not that ill after all, she can simply be discharged. However, the writer fails to follow his own observation through: if the patient's condition really does improve with contact, it would surely be natural to provide just that.

But what is unique about this file is that the discussion is *still* not over. Another note made on the same day by the locum comments on the transfer. Based on normal human behaviour it is likely that the locum wants to rectify things after his admonishment by the consultant – and at the same time backtrack on his earlier opposition in the notes:

> 11) Transfer note (locum NN). The patient is transferred today, [. . .] from ZZ to XX. The patient was in preventive care, hoping for a transfer to XX 8 days ago. The application was then turned down. She has now had a week more at ZZ, and has been put forward yet again for transfer to XX due to overcrowding. The undersigned had a short conversation with the patient on the day of the move. The patient seemed passive, had good eye contact, but there was little interaction otherwise. [. . .] The patient seems very unresponsive to medication. *The aim of the transfer*

to XX must be to get the patient to an improved level of mental functioning so that she doesn't have to be admitted again [italics added].

It is again noted that the transfer takes place due to overcrowding. At the same time the note sets up a target – a purpose – to get the patient to an *improved level of functioning*. This justifies the transfer as such: one could surely not object to the patient being helped towards an improved level of functioning? Yet the true, underlying purpose was quite different, that is, to take the pressure off an overcrowded ward. This internal lack of logic is characteristic and possibly instrumental in shaping a large proportion of the material from our own time: The writer is under pressure from so many divergent interests that the text simply has to show cracks.

THE PERSECUTED HOSPITAL

I came across more records in this period than in any other, in which suspicions were voiced that a patient was simulating. Beyond any medical realities that may lie behind this, one can also see that from the writer's perspective, simulation points in the right direction: What the hospital wants most of all is to be able to discharge the patient. The writer can become so obsessively suspicious, that even the patient's family is drawn into this *field of distrust*:

> 12) Since her discharge the hospital has received many telephone calls from the family, mostly the husband. The family have claimed that the patient was sent home too early, that she is incapable of taking adequate care of her xx-treatment etc.

According to the notes then, the family only "claimed"; where they could equally well have "made it clear". The writer's formulation undermines the possibility that the family may be right. Despite the rhetoric of the day, that everything will be "agreed together", the writer is merciless in deciding who amongst "us" is right. A little later we read:

> 13) The patient is still psychotic, but does not require special attention to diet, and does not need to be on a closed ward, and her present condition seems similar to that described in good periods between her stays at XX Hospital. *We question the discrepancy between her behaviour on the ward and how she was described by her family in the days before her admission.* This ought to be raised with the family in the near future. [italics added]

The statement "still psychotic" is undermined through three immediate modifications. And not least through the conjunction "psychotic, *but* . . .". The writer feels persecuted as a representative of the hospital by the family:

> 14 NN [family member] is very persistent when it comes to getting the patient in a more controlled environment, and I spend time with him explaining various issues around [the patient's] showing responsibility, to making agreements etc. [. . .] He [the family member] is very persistent and at times accusatory about the treatment offered. I believe this is more an expression of his despair in a difficult situation, than anything else.

We would normally expect words like "persistent" and "accusatory" to be used to describe the *patient*; here the internal hospital language spreads outside the hospital boundaries, to include the family, just as it did in the 1940s record in which the patient's father was classified as a pycnic.

The writer insists that the key phrases "showing responsibility" and "making agreements" need to be understood by the family: ". . . and I spend time with him explaining various issues . . .". The sympathetic interpretation of the family member's reaction being "more an expression of his despair in a difficult situation than anything else" is admittedly qualified through the addition of "I believe", but the modification does not seem to alter the statement in general. But what does the writer mean by "than anything else"? Does he mean something along the lines of "an understandable criticism seen from the family's point of view; but which, objectively speaking, is so unreasonable that there is no need to go into it"?

Genre-wise, the writer's arrogance is made possible here by the fact that from the beginning of the entry the family member is placed linguistically on a par with the role of the patient, a role for which separate rules of communication apply.

But in real terms the writer's authority is undermined, and a feeling of impotency surfaces. In some of the most recent records we looked at, the hospital seems to be under such pressure, that the conclusion drawn by the writer does not relate to the note's content. In the following example it is obvious that the writer does very little to align content and conclusion. In the age of the Dictaphone the writing moves so linearly – and without graphological trace – that the writer no longer sees the absence of cohesion in the text he produces:

15) This has led to a series of episodes in which she has impulsively and unpredictably acted out by hitting several fellow patients. She has also attacked some of the staff violently. For the last two days, the patient has been separated off, in the main, because of a couple of violent episodes, including hitting a nurse on the head with a soda bottle. She has bitten, kicked and lashed out. It is difficult to calm her in such situations, and on two occasions she has been medicated by force [. . .] There have now been three episodes during the last two days that must be described as serious. There have been no changes in the patient's medication during this phase. So it is with surprise we observe the dramatic deterioration that is taking place [. . .] *The only change to have happened round the patient is that her parents and ourselves have been able to cooperate on realistic discharge plans.* [italics added]

Here, the patient's "dramatic deterioration" is viewed with passive bewilderment. There is, as far as I have been able to ascertain from reading this patient's record, nothing up to this point to indicate any planned discharge. Yet the significance of this move is played down when the writer dismisses it as "The *only* change to have happened round the patient . . .". According to the writer, then, it seems there is no reason to think such a "minor detail" could have had any effect. The description that "[we] have been able to", also puts a positive slant on this information: the impossible is finally possible. But this linguistic utterance stands in sharp contrast to the content of the note elsewhere. And the patient reacts:

16) It seems the signalling of a future change is too difficult for the patient to handle, and that it has resulted in a worsening of her symptoms with dramatically more aggressive behaviour. Another possible explanation for the timing of this deterioration, is that the patient recently asked, on her own volition, for [an object of a particular delusion]. This is one of several occasions in which the patient has failed to get a response to her delusions. If we assume that her delusions help remodel a difficult and intolerable life situation in which she is undervalued as mother, partner, and worker, and that she creates an alternative delusional system in which she is one of the last people on earth to receive Our Lord's favour, when this falls apart it seems likely it explains her increased desperation and unease.

The writer's difficulty in creating cohesion and adequate explanations, is also reflected in the dissolving syntax towards the end of the note. The "if" at the start at the sentence is never resolved, instead the sentence changes direction with a new sub-clause beginning with the phrase "when this falls apart".

We have not found many instances in the text corpus of phrases like *"another possible explanation"*. This lends the text a sense of openness – it has generally been extremely rare to find traces in our material of such interpretive activity. Yet again, the interpretation of this patient's situation is carefully directed; the aim, to get her out of the hospital, is never lost sight of, no matter how the symptoms are explained.

The plans for the patient's discharge are presented in passing in her story. However, when another ward is to be burdened with the patient in question, the writer spends considerable effort in putting this as gently as possible to the new ward:

> 17) [. . .] However, it looks as if the approaching Easter also makes it very difficult to handle the patient at ZZ. It is difficult to get hold of extra staff and we have several people on sick leave at the moment. We are therefore forced to ask the emergency dept. for help in looking after this patient through Easter. It is, however, quite clear on our part that this is merely a request for temporary relief because of the patient's worsening symptoms, and because we have difficulty getting the required resources together.

The patient is returned and her condition deteriorates:

> 18) (discharge note psychologist NN) After the stay at ZZ was terminated a little earlier than planned due to crowding, the patient's condition has again deteriorated.

A connection is made here between the patient's poor condition and the lack of treatment on offer; although there is no conditional clause, the events follow each other in time. This has, as we have seen, been a common practice throughout the 100-year period: Causal connections are suggested, but without any direct markers which can be pointed to in retrospect. The note continues:

> 19) We have, over time, cooperated with her parents about possible solutions. The parents are adamant about trying to take their daughter home. This despite dramatic worsening of the patient's psychotic behaviour. She can attack personnel, unpredictably and totally without motive [. . .] We have therefore been obliged, out

of consideration for the safety of other patients and staff, to put the patient into iso-
lation for prolonged periods. The parents found this situation very difficult. [. . .]

The case for the patient's [immediate] discharge is strengthened since she
experiences the waiting time before her discharge as a massive burden accompanied with constant anxiety and desperation. What externally seems like a plan
designed to reassure, and possibly reduce the patient's delusions a little, becomes
for her like sitting in some kind of waiting room before an execution.

For a long time it has been our evaluation that there is no prospect of improvement for the patient at the hospital.

There is not a *single* argument presented in the *text* for the patient's discharge.
On what, then, does the writer base his formulation; "the case for the
patient's discharge is strengthened"? It seems in this entry that family pressure has won the day. Does the family, we may ask, have greater influence in
this period? Looking at the previous patient file it seems clear that opposite
was true; the hospital did not give in to the family, and even criticised them
in terms otherwise reserved for difficult patients. On the face of it, it seems
strange perhaps that these two records could reflect such directly opposing
attitudes, yet the pay-off in both situations is the same and is equally high;
the patient is removed from the system. Perhaps, in the age of the computer
which adds so much volume to the files, it has become easier to disguise
it when the focus of a record shifts from the best interests of the patient to
that of the hospital.

When the writer argues that "there is no prospect of improvement", his
attitude implicitly precludes any prospect of further discussion. When, one
might ask, was a decision made that maintaining the status quo did not
justify a continued hospital stay? The implied conclusion here is that since
there is no chance of improvement, the patient must leave the system. What
extraordinary pressure the writer is putting on the patient to improve! We
have already observed a certain irritation or hint of sarcasm in the material
from our own time, when, for example, the writer suggests that the patient
is "putting it on" because he sees the hospital as a nice place to stay.

The patient in the record above is indeed discharged, and takes her life
two days later. This is mentioned in passing, in reference to a conversation
with her father. The file ends:

20) I make an appointment with the father for me to call in 2 days to offer our help
again.

The content of the conversation that takes place two days later is not revealed. Does the conversation even take place? This last note in the file came under the heading "outpatient note", following the final "discharge note". There is nothing to mark that the patient has died. The death is well hidden, and the writer does not seem particularly keen on pointing it out.

And with this tragic conclusion the report comes to an end, as does our investigation of it.

One of the most pronounced impressions of the patient files from our time is the occasional *animosity* that surfaces in the description of patients. The writer draws a picture of a person against whom one needs to protect oneself; it is often hinted that a patient is an opportunist who is out to exploit the hospital situation; somebody who acts according to whim:

> 21) The patient is transferred from [. . .] but has come to a full stop at home [. . .] used larger doses of medicine than prescribed. Gave as reason that he was hearing voices again [. . .] Same symptoms that also led to his admission at V. He had come to a full stop there too, it was impossible to go any further with him.

We see here a new requirement. It is now necessary to "go further" with the patient; how different from the patient records at the turn of the century, in which notes would generally end with the patient being moved from B to C to D or vice versa, or with the standard formulations: "discharged cured"/"discharged recovered"/"discharged improved"/"discharged uncured"/"discharged dead". Yet there are innumerable cases in which the patient's "going further" certainly *does not* happen. This note continues:

> 22) [. . .] and bullied himself into being admitted, since he could not get by in his flat on his own [. . .] he discharged himself today.

It is also new that the patient is given the active role – he is no longer "discharged" but *discharges himself*. The writer has lost faith in the system's hold over the patient. He makes a passive record of the patient taking what he wants. The new concept here is of the patient *bullying himself into being admitted*. Another extraordinary example of institutional passivity. Where has the old self-assured authority gone? It seems the discourse of the writer is unwittingly dominated by non-psychiatric conditions. There is a shortage of resources in the mental health system, and the writer is faithful to whatever the current systems are. He never problematises them, but they become embedded in his discourse as paradoxes, at right angles to his stated intentions.

The following patient file contains a number of short notes that reveal indirectly how closed the hospital is – but in the 1980s "closed" no longer means that the hospital is difficult to get *out* of, rather that it protects itself from anyone getting *in*:

> 23) He heard and witnessed all these people shouting at him and chasing him. He ran through the forest at H. and every time he came to a street he saw "these people" standing there waiting to get him. He finally got a cab and escaped to his uncle in A. NN experiences the whole episode as real. [. . .] While at his uncle's house he saw a psychiatrist W., whom he asked for help to get into Gaustad. Application for admission was signed by Dr. W. When asked why he wants a stay at Gaustad, he is very vague. The only concrete thing he can say is that he needs help, in a safe place, to tackle his anxiety.

This is probably the first time we see the patient being asked what he expects from the hospital. The writer notes that the patient's answer is "very vague" on this point. It is not everyone's right to be admitted into Gaustad; it calls for proper motivation. Based on the textual fragments above it must be self-evident too that as a patient one is automatically cast in the role of opportunist, when one is faced with such firm but incoherent requirements of appropriate patient behaviour.

> 24) NN is sometimes difficult to work with on the ward. He expresses a need for help quite clearly, sees his angst as strenuous, but sabotages the treatment programmes that have been arrived at together.

The writer clearly find it important to stress that the treatment programmes have been arrived at "together". Yet no matter how democratic this may be, we never hear the patient's experience of this assumed cooperation.

> 25) His expressed aims for the stay have been somewhat varied, from being able to live in his flat alone, to moving to X country [. . .] We have continually tried to support him and offer him help in developing skills to live in his flat alone.

"To support him" is one of those positively charged expressions from the period that become very popular and which signal the writer's "good intentions" to the reader; but, as mentioned above, many of the positively charged expressions are undermined because the context works against them. Further on we read:

> 26) Because of his sabotaging of the ward programmes and the treatment on offer, it has sometimes appeared that A's [forename] main motivation for staying here has been to live as if in a hostel, to come to a laid table, to have no commitments and to have a nice time with the other "guests".

Here the writer seems perplexed as to the attraction, from the patient's perspective, of living a life "as if in a hostel". The writer is appealing to a moral code that the patient does not share. He feels misunderstood by the patient. Who wouldn't, he laments, want to have a cushy time? This offended tone *is* surprising and would have been unthinkable earlier.

> 27) With his primitive defences and poorly developed object relations but without psychotic tendencies, his personality is consistent with a badly functioning borderline patient.

Yet this description does not take into account that the man is a de facto tramp. In itself this note is not unlike the one from the 1890s which listed all the bad traits of a young convict. It continues:

> 28) On one hand he asks for help, and then when someone reaches out to offer it to him, he no longer wants it. *For the last ten years he has lived a life of no responsibility.* [italics added]

Once more one is taken aback by an absence of caring for the patient and of any understanding for his social situation. The man *has* for the greater part of the period been living as a tramp. To most people *"a life of no responsibility"* sounds more like a carefree playboy existence than a life spent without a roof over your head. The writer seems incapable of identifying with a social situation different to his own; he expects his own moral code to be shared by everyone, and yet this is no longer framed within the old ideology of the "moral treatment". The writer makes no attempt to discuss what might make a gainful human being; rather, his main priority is that the patient should not be a bother to the hospital. The moral values have, it seems, been narrowed down – if one believes in a fundamental equality. Everybody must now sign up to the writer's priorities.

The occupation of the young man whom we met in the 1890s, who was attributed with a long list of negative personality traits, was listed as *convict*. Being a convict, he was as convicts were expected to be. Today, the writer sets up a closeness between the patient and himself ("together we will"). When this closeness breaks, the writer turns and marks a more aggressive form of distancing. The writer fails to see his own paradoxical attitude, yet he probably perceives himself as far more considerate than his predecessors.

Sometimes it is emphasised that the hospital has the best of intentions in its actions. As we see here:

> 29 (1990) These two conversations took on an introductory character which gave us the opportunity to get to know each other *with a view to the best possible treatment outcome for the patient.* [italics added]

Has anyone ever, one wonders, wanted "a *worst* possible treatment outcome" for a patient? This statement is void of any real content, but functions as an invocation for the writer himself. Alternatively, the writer may be placing signals in his text that will look positive should the patient ever use his right of access to the patient file. The writer may, for example, express huge disappointment with the patient later, but he *has* made it absolutely clear that "we have agreed *together*", and that the hospital has always aimed at "the *best* possible outcome".

As time passes, however, the patient has considerable frustration poured over him. The asylum has simply not got space for him – but neither has anyone else.

> 30 [After various episodes, including an escape.] Today we have an extensive discussion about the continued treatment of F. [forename] on the ward. It is clear that he has considerable problems in keeping appointments and sticking to the goals that he himself has been involved in setting. At the same time, we have not been able to see any conclusive psychotic symptoms during his stay. Condition is characterised more by impulsive behaviour, a lack of structure and an inability to take care of himself. His motivation for staying on the ward fluctuates wildly, and it is our opinion that he is capable of taking more responsibility for what happens to him. We have therefore chosen to transfer him to par. 4 in Law of [. . .] and we are also drawing up a clear treatment programme with him today, including penalties for breach of agreements.

[. . .] patient has, during his stay on the ward, presented very few symptoms beyond [his having] an extremely evasive and rather unstructured personality. He has continually undermined the goals he has taken part in setting up and has additionally contributed to a very destructive environment, as he seems to be one of the leaders of a drug culture amongst 4 fellow patients. *Consequently a continued stay seems to be of little benefit to F.* [italics added]

The end of the note strikes us as rather outrageous; the patient has, on the whole, expressed a desire to stay at the hospital. His occasional running away would have been met with less surprise in a previous time, when patients were not faced with the same demands of logic as they are now. In reality it is not for F that "a continued stay is of little benefit"; it is the *hospital* that has no idea where to put him, yet the writer turns this into F's problem. In the quote above it is noticeable that the writer stresses that various "choices" are available: "we therefore choose to transfer . . ."

All the files from the fourth period are consistently well presented and structured, made up of well-written texts that are neatly laid-out. However the coherence of the notes is not always as impressive. When external conditions take over, the notes immediately dissolve and argumentation becomes rooted in priorities other than those first suggested. The following example will be our last of this type of incoherent internal motivation:

31) Admission note [. . .] on admission he is anxiety ridden and we endeavour to make him safe in the environment.

14 days later: (discharge note (Doctor MM)) Because of the space situation on the ward, we have to discharge the patient today. He took the news very well and said it was just as well.

What is remarkable is the importance laid on the patient's feeling that it was "just as well". In previous times, we might also have expected something like "the patient has no awareness of his illness". Yet here there seems to be no evaluation in the final note, as to whether the goals set earlier in the file have been realised. Have they succeeded, or not, in making him feel safe in the environment? The "space situation" is all that is commented upon (the ever-faithful writer shies away being more explicit and describing the problem as a "space *shortage*"). We are told that "He took the news very well"; but in relation to what? – That he was short-changed perhaps, as regards to his being made safe in the environment? Perhaps, it is as a balm to the writer's bad conscience that the patient is given the last word; "just as well". How much more pride was there in the writer who wrote the discharge note at the turn of the century: "often abusive and angry, indecent in her speech, is at departure pleasant, happy and smiling and curtsies when bidding her farewells".

USE OF LANGUAGE

Also new in our time, are the sporadic references to a kind of meta-reflection on the medical terminology in the patient records:

> 32) [She] describes her [own] thoughts in medical terms and can describe the progress and development of these, and then concludes the conversation by claiming that the undersigned is a Satanist [. . .]

The fact that the patient is using medical terms to describe her thoughts is left uncommented upon. The writer does not embark upon the subject of shared language versus diverging sociolects.

In the following example the patient attempts to speak in the language of the "other":

> 33) He says himself that he has had psychotic experiences. He says he has felt ambivalent towards antipsychotic medication.

Medical language is now a shared language. One may wonder whether the use of this language results in fuller descriptions of situations than, for example, the religious language formulations of the turn of the century. Different times; different languages. In the example above, it is the writer's linguistic field that has spread to that of the patient.

But in the 1990s there also is a definite tendency on behalf of the writer to attempt to describe the patient's language in a more linguistically precise way. The word "syntax" is now commonplace in the writer's vocabulary, and the writer generally gives an impression of greater theoretical knowledge about language:

> 34) He answers questions, but his language is affected by disturbances of a formal as well as a content related character.

35) The paranoid ideas of the patient are still prominent, he is incoherent and associates very fast and incomprehensibly. In periods every single sentence is syntactically broken.

COMPASSION

Long gone are the chronicle-like family presentations of the type "father a drunkard, mother suffers from bad nerves". In the following example family members are only mentioned according to their *function* in relation to the daily activities of the patient.

36) The patient's parents are presently on [. . .] holiday at their cottage, and it was the intention that the patient's brother and he should travel up tomorrow.

The main function of the patient's brother in this narrative is as an actor in the patient's life; he is the person who can facilitate the planned holiday. Thus, the fact that the patient has a brother is only mentioned in passing, and only in relation to the bearing he has on the story. The patient's relationships have, in our time, lost their absolute value; they are now mentioned as and when the context calls for it. This marks a significant cultural shift in the patient record.

Throughout the entire 100-year period writers have resisted suggesting that the behaviour of the patient is socially conditioned. In the following note the writer highlights the patient's cultural difference. The patient in question is a Southern European, and his differentness is not so great as to cause much complication:

37) He praises the undersigned profusely [. . .] It is evident that he wishes to placate the undersigned, *while his expressions must also be somewhat culturally conditioned.* [italics added]

It is interesting that the writer finds it necessary to include this *relativising* piece of information. We have seen many examples of condescension to, for instance, servant girls, and heightened textual interest given to people from the higher echelons of society, but the writer has never hitherto made the patient's cultural background subject to reflection.

We also come across numerous examples in recent material, of deeply empathic conversations between doctor and patient of the type I have so often admired in previous periods. This may manifest itself in both content as well as in more linguistic expressions:

> 38) We discuss at length concepts like faith, truth and God. During this he becomes increasingly sceptical about whether it is right for him to give in to the fateful messages of the voices. He seems to accept my suggestion that he should be as free as possible in relation to both internal and external forces.

Extraordinarily, the note's generalising introduction, "we discuss at length", seems to be confirmed in what follows: not for a moment does the writer give the impression that he possesses a higher truth than the patient in their discussion.

Occasionally, the writer is not frightened of expressing the paradoxical nature of his practice. A cure may, for example, make life less meaningful on occasion:

> 39) He occasionally falls into religious ponderings and harbours ideas of being Jesus. On the whole this is however not very prominent, and, as mentioned, face to face he is largely unpsychotic and competent. [. . .] He says he becomes emotionally empty from taking Hibanil. When asked what he means by this, he explains that the idea for example that he is Jesus disappears and then life is poorer.

> 40) We carry on talking about death for a while. I say that if one wishes to be dead, one has to be rather sad or find life difficult. The patient then says that she is possibly a little sad. She goes on to say that she feels it is normal to wish she was dead. The patient is asked what she thinks we can do to help her. The patient says that she doesn't think we can do very much for her.

The patients' attitudes here are not subjected to moralising, and the writer enters into a discussion with the patient on a topic in which neither of them is has thematic authority. The writer is also careful to note that the patient's final, bitter comment has arisen from a question. The content is firmly attributed to the patient, but the writer's loyalty to this patient allows him to express an unspoken and also touching meeting of minds; the meaninglessness of life and the hospital's shortcomings are insights shared by both parties.

We also continue to find examples of textual fragments of the type "synopsis of a story", a form we have observed throughout the entire 100-year period. The following note completes a very long file that covers numerous stays in the hospital:

> 41 (Outpatient note) On Friday [. . .]. the ward was phoned by the newspaper delivery girl. Recently she had been invited in by the patient for an occasional cup of coffee. Last time she saw him he had been lying on the sofa doubled up with stomach pains. She had wanted him to go to A&E, but the patient objected. When she did not see him for a few days, and the patient did not appear, she called the police who went into the flat where they found him dead on the sofa.

What is the purpose of such a story? We are immediately struck by the concrete details. The previous medical history loses some of its value. The note signals little more than the writer's interest in an old, and in his way, dear acquaintance. A story is simply being brought to a conclusion; such a contrast to the suicide mentioned earlier in this chapter, which was made invisible.

In this period we also find notes that are totally timeless in their format; notes that are almost representative of any period:

> 42) 7th stay, Admission note. Pt. gets up around 9 every day, eats breakfast alone after having given the cat some milk. Feels that the morning is the worst part of the day.

The detail of the cat getting its milk makes the reader suddenly *see* the situation. It is like the tiny details in a realistic novel that the structuralist can never fit into his structural reading (as Roland Barthes points out in *The Reality Effect*), but which, for that very reason, give the reader greater enjoyment. It is the nugget of information that exists *for* no purpose in particular.

We have seen that there is a place for great existential questions as well as small everyday details in the patient records; both are essential aspects of being human.

We also come across several almost formulaic expressions in this file, giving voice to the frustration at the pain suffered by patients, as well as the hopelessness of the hospital situation:

> 43) [In ref. to marriage conversation] The situation is such now, that it is difficult to be optimistic of further progress. If there had been sufficient treatment resources this patient in acute psychotic phase should have had help through frequent

individual conversations to work through an enormous guilt problem, longing and loss in relation to parents and siblings.

What is new is that the reflection of the writer on the absence of treatment programs: ". . . if there had been sufficient treatment resources". But what is also new to this period is the assessment of a situation in terms of *optimism*, or, in this case, the *lack* of it. In previous times such vocabulary was avoided. This does not mean writers have never reflected on this question before, but it has not been manifest in their writing. Perhaps this note represents a rather courageous criticism of the system?

ACCESS TO RECORDS

I have only once, in the entire material, come across any mention of a patient reading his own file.

> 44) K [forename] has also asked to see the file in question from his stay at DXX. He has seen it, and as he read it through he smiled several times and said "I shan't comment on what it says here, but I understand why you see it this way." It was impossible to get him to be specific about what he was reacting to.

I expected, as many psychiatric professionals probably did, that the legal ruling on patients' right to access their records might skew the writing. To my astonishment, I have not been able to confirm any significant change. This may be because in focusing on such a wide variety of factors, I have failed to look specifically at this one, and that a closer study might reveal such a difference. Alternatively the corpus may be too small. But it is also true that the writers have always been mindful of a wide of number considerations in writing psychiatric records. Earlier patient records were based on a shared norm that was far removed from the patient. In our time, on the other hand, we see a writer trying to convince another ward that it must take care of the patient (one writer against another). The written text has always been restrained and obscuring. Avoiding the risk of offending a patient who might, at some future date, inspect the record, will only ever be one of the writer's many considerations. The respect or fear of the official inspectorate and its possible intrusion remains a factor in this period too. This occasionally results in lengthy notes detailing how plans for compulsory interventions have been communicated to the patient:

45) He has understood the decision from [date] [about compulsory medication]. During the conversation he scrunched up the decision sheet, yet unfolded it and took it away with him when the conversation was over. He has since written a small message in the top corner of the sheet, clearly indicating he wants to complain about the decision to the hospital. But he has not yet formulated a written complaint. Our assessment is such as to make this unnecessary, and we have interpreted his protest of screwing up of the sheet and throwing it away from him on receiving the decision, as equivalent to a complaint to the national physician [sic]. The decision is being sent by car to the national physician today, so that a representative from the county authorities will come to speak with [patient's name] about it.

Here the writer uses all his skill as a good storyteller to show that he acts within the letter of the law, even though it appears that he doesn't quite know the correct titles of the relevant state officials. No doubt this is more of a driving factor for him than any notion of adapting his text to the potential sensitivities of a patient. After 100 years of practice, the writer is also smart enough to adjust his wording so that it will mean one thing within the context of the hospital, but something more diluted in the real world outside, should that prove necessary.

__NL__

__NL____NL__

Conclusion

A DOUBLE NARRATIVE

Before I began on my analysis of the material from Gaustad Hospital I had already formed an abstract notion of the patient records as a double and paradoxical form of communication:

> A patient tells their story to a note-writing doctor; the story is in other words recorded by a person other than the one producing it. The writer does not share the teller's perception of reality – particularly when this is dominated by psychopathological manifestations – but he will nonetheless aim to record what the patient presents as faithfully as possible, so as to keep a clear distinction between description and evaluation. The writer evaluates the story produced and forms a picture of the narrator behind it, both as he listens and afterwards. The writer doubts the referential content of the story he himself is recording, but at the same time he will try to find the sources of the narrative production of the story. (Aaslestad, 1995, p. 11).

This model seems, after going through the Gaustad material, to have held true. In retrospect I have come to realise that there is essentially no difference between psychiatric records and other medical case notes: both are sustained by a narrative potential. The doctor and patient will always have different perceptions of reality during the production of the story, in respect of the case's pathological aspect. A great deal of the international literature dealing with hospital case notes points to this same duality. Many researchers see the doctor–patient relationship as analogous to the reader–text relationship. We have remarked previously how Kathryn Montgomery Hunter problematises

171

the notions of text and reader from a poststructuralist point of view not dissimilar to our own. The notion of "patient as a text" is used by her as a metaphor in order to describe processes that evolve during the encounter between patient and doctor. Let us for a moment return to the analogy, as it appears in "reality", in medical practice. Rita Charon's observations are representative:

> The patient tells the story in roughly the same way the author creates a work. The doctor listens to that story, decoding it or interpreting it in roughly the same way that a reader makes sense of a written work. (Charon, 1992, p. 117)

One essential difference must necessarily be that "readers" interpret stories according to strict rules of causality and significance; rules which, according to Charon, the patient may not recognise as his own. This duality is important to foreground. But even in the practical, everyday medical situation, the analogy between medicine and literature is too simplistic. The doctor (reader) meets the patient (text), but every time the doctor (reader) has a further consultation with his patient (text), beyond their first meeting, the doctor continues to form more opinions based on the *text about* the patient that already exists. And this text can play a significant role in the patient's future. Indeed, over time "the patient" often becomes little more than a text. Thus the title of this book, *The Patient as Text*, should not be seen as merely metaphorical, but as an exploration of that separate, but very real, aspect of the patient which *is* the written text.

CLASSICISM VS ROMANTICISM

The inherent opposition between the patient's and doctor's understanding of the illness can be placed in the wider framework of the history of ideas. According to Charon, medical students of physiology and anatomy learn about the "ideal form of the human body". Illnesses are defined as *deviations* from this ideal. All patients are seen against a background of a perfect form. A universally accepted understanding of the ideal or normal body constitutes the platform for any meeting with the patient. Attempts by the medical profession to recover an ideal state that has been lost, is both a conservative and heroic project. To Charon, the field of clinical medicine is not as *linear* and positivistic as is sometimes presented, but *cyclical* in its attempts at returning people to their previous states. To call this writing classical, foregrounds its timeless and normative nature. As such, medical science is, according to Charon (1992, p. 119f), not so much science as a platonic longing for a well-proportioned truth and beauty. This may seem rather outlandish, and at first glance less relevant to "our" branch of medicine. It is easy to see the difficult position in which psychiatry is placed, when it is forced to define psychiatric illness against a background of absolute notions of "normality". But it is precisely this position in which note-writers have presumably found themselves, whether or not they are ideologically comfortable with these notions themselves. So once again we end up vindicating Foucault's ideas of the definition of madness as dictated by a need to maintain the supremacy of common sense.

Even if some "case-stories" end gloriously with the recovery of an ideal state, the majority testify to the treatment's failure. It can seem that the ultimate aim for the note-writer is that he is able to say: "I did as well as anyone could". Charon's focus is, of course, general medicine, but we have observed precisely the same trend in psychiatric records, and at times the sentiment of "we have done our level best" is used to obscure the final defeat exacted by the illness on both the patient and medical profession.

Charon asserts that when the doctor has taken the step of instigating clinical action, the story has to be told in such a way as to justify that action. This is something we have encountered frequently in the Gaustad records. In my material these justifications often appear in the form of notes referring to a marked improvement in the patient, until, that is, regressions start to appear. Yet this is a tendency seen mainly in the files of patients who have had electroshock treatment or lobotomies. Nowadays, when medication has become the norm, the writer's justifications of his own actions appear more balanced; the patient's reactions to the medication do not eliminate interest in other aspects of the patient. On the other hand, the writer's anxiety about being left with a patient on the ward for whom there is no bed, seems central in the story's progression. Simultaneously, we have observed that the writer is extremely cautious about suggesting any clear-cut cause and effect: he merely offers inferences that will be open to interpretation depending on future developments. That we find less of the kind of justification discussed by Charon, is, of course, also because there has, throughout history, been less clinical intervention in the psychiatric hospital. The prescribed treatment for psychiatric illness in the early days was "calm", beyond which there was "nothing to be done".

The patient's story belongs, according to Charon, to the Romantic tradition, which venerates expressiveness. The patient is not particularly concerned with the universal. He wants to get better and wants to be heard, added to which he wants the listener to give purpose to his story. The patient is full of emotion and spontaneity, and he meets the doctor who seeks the perfect form.[39]

It is important to emphasise that the distance between the doctor and patient is neither superficial nor built on misunderstandings that can easily be swept aside. On the contrary; the distance is essential and unbridgeable. This comes through in the example at the opening of this book, in which the female lobotomy patient expresses anger at the doctor's misunderstanding of her responses. To minimise this distance Charon suggests encouraging doctors to make greater use of both the professionals' and the patients' individual language patterns. Much of the international literature supports Charon's demand that the patient's universe should feature more prominently in written records.[40] Scepticism towards the patient's subdued or virtually invisible role in the story about himself, is described clearly in the polemic article "Is there a person in this case?"[41] in which the authors conclude that today's patient files often use degrading terminology, encourage hasty categorisations, and can sometimes exclude the voice of the patient

---

39 In her more recent book, Charon gives a different emphasis to the distinction between the (individual) romanticism of the patient and the (universal) classicism of medical science: "What distinguishes narrative knowledge from universal or scientific knowledge is its ability to capture the singular, irreplaceable, or incommensurable" (Charon, 2006, p. 45). The narratological is defined as something outside the field of science. This distinction is probably a useful delineation in the medical context, but when narrative knowledge is not placed inside scientific knowledge, the human sciences are excluded; no doubt unintentionally, but in such a way as to make it more difficult and less encouraging to enter into a fruitful dialogue on one's own scientific premises.

40 The following quote from A Kleinman's *Rethinking Psychiatry* is a suitable example: "To fully appreciate the sick person's and the family's experience, the clinician must first piece together the illness narrative as it emerges from the patient's and the family's complaints as explanatory models; then he or she must interpret it in light of the different modes of illness meanings-symptoms symbols, culturally salient illnesses, personal and social contexts" (Kleinman, 1988, p. 49).

41 This article is by WF Monroe, WL Holleman and M Cline Hollman in *Literature and Medicine*. 1992; **11**: 45–63. Its title is amusing, referring as it does to modern literary criticism and to Stanley Fish's article "Is there a text in this class?" Fish was already critical in the 1970s of the tendencies in literary criticism to dissolve and ignore the literary work.

altogether. The article points out that the use of numerical data comes at the expense of storytelling; the patient needs to be rescued as a "cultural text" and liberated from the identity of a mere "biochemical body". Such sentiments seem to have grown more common in the last few years. As a consequence one might ask the question, as JC Frich and P Fugelli (2005) did in their article "Should the patient be allowed to write in his own file?" Their conclusion is far from unfavourable to the idea. But not everybody would see a purpose to extending the scope of the patient record in this way. In Einar Kringlen's chapter about note-writing in his textbook (1977), we see an underlying insistence that note-writing is supposed to hold a world of fixed components in place. There is less room in Kringlen than in Charon for the patient. Perhaps this is inherent in psychiatry itself; more than in any other field of medicine, those involved in the world of psychiatry are also carriers of society's morals and sense of order (cf. the "moral treatment" discussed earlier).

Kringlen also underlines the medical-scientific importance of the establishment of the doctor/patient relationship *before* any writing actually takes place: "'let me conduct the anamnesis myself' a well-known consultant said to the student" (Kringlen 2005, p. 101). Kringlen stresses that even the first interview with the patient should, ideally, have a therapeutic effect: "The psychiatric interview is a remarkable instrument. The doctor enjoys enormous trust and often gets information that nobody else could get." (ibid) Again in his textbook, Kringlen's anonymous "well-known consultant", who so clearly marks his authority towards the equally anonymous "student", brings to mind – with his aura of safe, natural authority – the doctor-role that Foucault sketched in *Madness and Civilization*: Based on the notion of family and children centred around the paternal authority, the doctor finds his healing power.

THE ELECTRONIC PATIENT RECORD AND PLAIN LANGUAGE

As far back as the 1960s, we find academic articles on effective note-taking as well as analysis of hospital records. The earliest contributions on computer programming reveal what is, with hindsight, a touching faith in scientific progress. For example, in an article from 1971, P Kolstad and K Nordbye distinguish between their forward-looking doctor colleagues who welcome automisation, and the backward-looking ones who have faith in the outdated, *handwritten* patient report. Using electronic tools, the authors wanted to tackle the lack of order and structure that characterises dictation into a Dictaphone. But in the midst of this progress-optimism, one also finds a clear sense of disquiet over the difficulties of transferring verbal cognition onto automated computer programs. For example, in his 1994 article, C-F Bassøe underlines that the "automatic analysis of natural language [is] however one of the most difficult unsolved problems within information technology." (p. 1974). A research group at Ullevål Hospital (Solberg *et al.*, 1995) investigating internal admission notes, concluded that the notes were frequently inadequate, and went on to express frustration over the problems of measuring quality:

> The second important discovery was that we found it impossible to develop consistent criteria by which to measure the quality of patient files. *The study showed that different doctors' opinions on the quality of the same file varied to such an extent, that it was impossible to use this information in any scientifically useful way.* [. . .] It is thought provoking and also troubling that we, as providers of health care, find it impossible to make a useful measurement of the quality of the most important documentation of our work, namely the patient file. (Solberg *et al.*, 1995, p. 489, italics added)

Despite its being tempting, in retrospect, to smile wryly at the optimism of the 60s and 70s at how comprehensive, reliable and simple the electronic records would be in a few years, one may conversely feel some admiration for the eagerness with which they engaged with the most difficult questions of note-writing; how much, for example, can be expressed in standardised forms, and how much remains as more or less unique and non-reductible narrative? These questions still seem relevant today. In their article "The electronic medical record and the 'story stuff': a narrativistic model"[42] Kay and Purves try to understand the structure of so-called free text in a "computer-based medical record system":

> Rather than regard «free text» as a messy embarrassment to perfect design, or as a last resort to be tolerated when coded forms of formal clinical representation fail, we see it as essential. [. . .] In many systems the so-called «free text» is the most useful part of a clinical record. (Kay and Purves 2004, p. 187)

---

42 In Greenhalgh T, Hurwitz B (eds). *Narrative Based Medicine. Dialogue and Discourse in Clinical Practice.* London; 2004, pp. 185–201.

The authors are convinced that narratology – in its widest etymological definition (ibid) – can offer solutions to this problem.[43] At the same time they understand why psychiatry has, so far, shown such limited interest in electronic patient files; "their particular focus being too discursive to be easily formalised" (ibid). At the time of writing there is no reason to question this conclusion. On the contrary, one may imagine that insights into the psychiatric record may have transferable value to the medical note in general, and thereby also to any electronic varieties.

The majority of Norwegian articles that explicitly investigate the medical record, rarely reflect on the meaning of language itself. But there are exceptions. In an article with what seems a promising title; "Good records mean good medicine" by Magne Nylenna (1992), the author looks at the shortcomings in files that can lead to problems in the case of a complaint. Nylenna concludes that "both the accuracy of data recorded and the level of communication between record users, improve when the language used is *plain, clear and unambiguous*" (p. 3562, italics added). At first glance, it is perhaps tempting to agree with this, but in practice a complex and multifaceted reality is not always best served by simpler language; indeed we have seen excellent examples of notes in which the patient's speech has been presented in both complex and original ways, that must have taken considerable intellectual input to achieve. And we have also seen textual fragments, as the last example in the first period – written in a very uncomplicated and symmetric style. In other words: there are times when a complex linguistic mode of expression might be as appropriate as something simple.

The issue of simplicity and clarity may have been easier to evaluate if there had been a division between vocabulary and syntax. In the material from our own time we have seen that the writer sometimes reflects the patient's peculiar use of syntax. Yet simultaneously as records display greater awareness of syntax, they also develop their own syntactical peculiarities. In

---

43 I have also encountered the same positive attitude to a narratological input at the National Centre for Electronic Patient Records, financed by The Research Council of Norway. (Can, for example, the switch between iterative and singulative narration be a factor in delineating the sphere of "free text"?) On the other hand, the "new narratology" (so called by Iversen and Skov Nielsen) is more concerned with the contextual and interpretative, rather than the taxonomies that classic structural narratology looked for. This disjointedness shows how heterogeneous the modern field of literary criticism can appear; although this need not be a hindrance in the further use of narratological insights in the development of the electronic patient file.

our own time we see so-called anacoluthons much more frequently; that is, statements that start one way grammatically but finish as though the sentence had begun quite differently. Although, common in casual speech, this is unforgivable in a written text since it undermines the logical connections between statements. The use of the Dictaphone as well as the PC have a tendency to produce less stringent sentence structures.

FINALLY

Our historical journey through the medical records of Gaustad Hospital has revealed a fascinating breadth of narrative forms. Several styles that might normally be regarded as peculiarly literary (almost avant garde-ish) reveal themselves here to be everyday "tools" for the writers of psychiatric reports. At other times we have seen borrowings from popular literature. But irrespective of such writing strategies, the notes are surprisingly faithful to what might, at the time of their writing, be seen as society's more conservative ideologies.

The research consisted of a close reading of around 150 records from a 100-year period at Gaustad hospital. I have restricted my investigation to the methods of storytelling. Gérard Genette's narratology and Barthes', Kristeva's and Bakhtin's understanding of intertextuality have informed my textual analysis as methodological paradigms, yet without it seeming necessary at every turn to foreground the specific methodological apparatus.

Now, as we near the end, reader and author may both feel the need to see some larger patterns. Our four main periods were headed only with their historical dates. It might have been tempting to divide the findings of this research into sections that reflect changes of approach: For example; "Static and unchanging," for the turn of the twentieth century; "respectful distance" for the 1920s, "generalisation and suspicion" 1940s and 50s, the "optimistic focus on the illness itself" in the 1970s; and maybe the "self-righteous insularity" of own times, etc. But we shall resist the temptation of concluding with such simplified résumés. These would, at any rate, need to be modified to account for individual writers' peculiarities. Besides which, any overarching through-lines would both obscure the fact that the research is based on a fairly limited body of material, and detract from the synchronous dimension of the material.

The patient is made audible and visible in the records via a repertoire of basic techniques available to the writer. These are almost infinitely varied. We have tried to identify the possible effects of different narrative techniques, why some are preferred above others, and how the historical context affects the choice of technique, as well as the basic structure of the record itself.

I have been surprised at how texts, even at the smallest micro-level, often seem to reflect facets of the contemporary historical context, beyond the boundaries of what one might expect when looking at the factual content of a note. The writer belongs to his time, yet must simultaneously be able to reflect on his position, before anyone else "beats him to it" and draws conclusions other than those he intends. In a way it is that simple and that complicated.

At the beginning of this chapter I pointed to the duality of the patient/ doctor encounter; the disparity of the experience of doctor and patient. This double perspective has been analysed in various ways, but the majority of authors discussing this topic seem to feel that a stronger relationship between the patient and doctor should be expressed in records. It may seem overly sentimental to draw special attention here to the great value of being patient-focused, but such a focus has, of course, been at the very heart of our research, looking as we have at ways in which the patient becomes visible in the psychiatric record.

Throughout the material, there have been writers who occasionally let themselves get carried away by the joy of storytelling. Despite the "hermeneutics of suspicion" that have naturally governed large portions of our research, I could not, as a reader, fail to admire the vast repertoire of style and form represented in the written files.

Despite the potential and pleasure of the text however, against the constant pressure of an underlying madness, the files respond with a depiction of life which is ultimately too systematised, and far from other textual portraits. And in the end, if proximity to dangerous topics becomes too difficult to handle, the text responds with its surest technique: Silence.

Bibliography

Aaslestad P. Den psykiatriske sykejournalen. Noen genrebetraktninger, med glimt fra Knut Hamsuns Vinderen-opphold 1945. In: Johnsen EB, editor. *Virkelighetens forvaltere. Norsk Sakprosa. Første bok.* Oslo; 1995, pp. 11–22.

Aaslestad P. *Narratologi. En innføring i anvendt fortelleteori.* Oslo; 1999.

Austad A-K, Ødegaard Ø. *Gaustad sykehus gjennom hundre år.* Oslo; 1956.

Bakhtin M. Du discours romanesque. In: *Esthétique et théorie du roman.* Paris; 1978.

Barthes R. Théorie du texte. In: *Encyclopedia Universalis.* Paris; 1973: 1013–17.

Barthes R. L'effet du réel. In: *Communications.* 1968 ; 11 : 84–9.

Bassøe C-F. Automatisk analyse av journaltekst. *J Norweg Med Assoc.* 1994; **17**(114): 1974–6.

Booth W. *The Rhetoric of Fiction.* Chicago and London; 1973.

Charon R. To build a case: Medical histories as traditions in conflict. *Literature and Medicine.* 1992; **11**(Spring): 115–32.

Charon R. *Narrative Medicine: Honoring the Stories of Illness.* Oxford; 2006.

Engebretsen E. *Barnevernet som tekst. Nærlesning av 15 utvalgte journaler fra 1950 – og 1980-tallet.* Oslo; 2006.

Felman S. "Turning the screw of interpretation". In: Felman S, editor. *Literature and Psychoanalysis.* New Haven, CT; 1978.

Fjellstad K, Isaksen TO, Frich JC. Kunst i den medisinske grunnutdanningen. *J Norweg Med Assoc.* 2003; **16**: 2316–18.

Forster EM. *Aspects of the Novel.* London; 1960.

Foucault M. *Madness and Civilization. A History of Insanity in the Age of Reason* (trans. R Howard). London and New York; 1964/1989.

Frich JC. Medisin som litterær virksomhet. *J Norweg Med Assoc.* 2003; **17**: 2474–6.

Frich JC, Fugelli P. Bør pasienter kunne skrive i egen journal? *J Norweg Med Assoc* 2005; **125**: 918.

Galioni EF, Adams FH, Tallman FF. Intensive treatment of back-ward patients: A controlled pilot study. *Am J Psychiatr* 1953; **109**: 576.

Genette G. Discours du récit. In: *Figures III*. Paris; 1972.

Greenhalgh T, Hurwitz B, editors. *Narrative Based Medicine: dialogue and discourse in clinical practice*. London; 2004.

Hamsun K. *På gjengrodde stier*. Samlede verker, bind 15. Oslo; 1956.

Hansen T. *Prosessen mot Hamsun*. Oslo; 1978.

Helman C. *Suburban Shaman: tales from medicine's frontline*. London; 2006.

Hydle I. Tradisjon og funksjonalitet i medisinsk tekst. Om pasienters og legers tolkning. In: Johnsen EB, editor. *Forbildets forbilder. Norsk sakprosa. Andre bok*. Oslo; 1996.

Iversen S, Skov Nielsen H, editors. *Narratologi*. Århus; 2004.

Kay S, Purves I. Medical records and other stories: a narratological framework. *Methods Inf Med*. 1996; **35**: 72–87.

Kelstrup A. Sosial kontroll av sinnssyke: Fra dårekiste til psykokjemi. In: Kringlen E, editor. *Psykiatri og historie*. Oslo; 1977, pp. 86–100.

Kirkebæk B. *Letfærdig og løsagtig – kvindeanstalten på Sprogø 1923–1961*. Holte; 2004.

Kleinman A. *Rethinking Psychiatry. From cultural category to personal experience*. New York; 1988.

Kolstad P, Nordbye K. Et system for automatisk databehandling av medisinske journaler. *J Norweg Med Assoc*. 1971; **91**: 405–9.

Kringlen E (ed). *Psykiatri og historie*. Oslo; 1977.

Kringlen E. *Psykiatriens samtidshistorie*. Oslo; 2001.

Kringlen E. *Psykiatri*. Oslo; 2005.

Kristeva J. Fra en identitet til en annen. In: A Kittang (mfl). *Moderne litteraturteori*. Oslo; 1991.

Kundera M. Discours de Jérusalem: le roman et l'Europe. In: *L'Art du roman*. Paris; 1986; pp. 194–9.

Langfeldt G, Ødegaard Ø. *Den rettspsykiatriske erklæring om Knut Hamsun*. Oslo; 1978.

Larsen, K. Journaler analysert med litteraturvitenskapelig lupe. *J Norweg Med Assoc*. 2008; **45**(8).

Malterud K. Språklige teknikker kan avdekke skjult informasjon i konsultasjonen. *J Norweg Med Assoc*. 1990; **25**(110): 3257–65.

McNay L. *Foucault. A Critical Introduction*. Cambridge; 1994.

Monroe WF, Holleman WL, Cline Holleman M. Is there a person in this case? *Lit Med.* 1992; 11: 45–63.

Montgomery K. *How Doctors Think: Clinical Judgment and the Practice of Medicine.* Oxford; 2006.

Montgomery Hunter K. *Doctors' Stories. The narrative structure of medical knowledge.* Princeton, NJ; 1991.

Nessa J. From a medical consultation to a written text. 1 Transcribing the doctor-patient dialogue. *Scand J Prim Health Care.* 1995; 13: 83–8.

Nylenna M. Gode journaler er god medisin. *J Norweg Med Assoc.* 1992; 28(112): 3560–5.

Olié JP, Spadone C. *Les nouveaux visages de la folie.* Paris; 1993.

Rees L. Physical characteristics of the schizophrenic patient. In: Richter D, editor. *Schizophrenia: somatic aspects.* London; 1957.

Retterstøl N. Gaustad Sykehus – historien fra planlegging frem til kommuneovertagelsen i 1985. In: Retterstøl N, editor. *Gaustad Sykehus 140 år.* Oslo; 1995.

Rosenbaum B, Sonne H. *Det er et bånd der taler: analyser af sprog og krop i psykosen.* København; 1979.

Sandberg O. *Klinisk Femtenaarsberetning fra Gaustad Asyl.* Kristiania; 1871.

Scharffenberg J. Article in *The Journal of the Norwegian Medical Association.* 1908.

Skålevåg SA. *Fra normalitetens historie – Sinnssykdom 1870–1920.* Rokkansenteret, rapport 10. Bergen; 2003.

Solberg E *et. al.* Journalen – innhold, forventning og kvalitet. En studie av 100 indremedisinske innkomstjournaler. *J Norweg Med Assoc.* 1995; 4(115): 488–9.

Stensland, P. Fortellingen i sykejournalen *J Norweg Med Assoc.* 2007; 127: 2268–9.

White H. Figuring the nature of the times deceased: literary theory and historical writing. In: Cohen R, editor. *The Future of Literary Theory.* London; 1989, pp. 19–43.

Østvold. Om privatforpleining af sindssyge. *Tidsskrift for Praktisk Medicin.* 1899; 205–10.